I0828316

Mentoring by Design

Mentoring by Design

Mentoring and Discipling Through Missional Small Groups

EDWARD R. MARTON

Foreword by Duane A. Anders

WIPF & STOCK · Eugene, Oregon

MENTORING BY DESIGN
Mentoring and Discipling Through Missional Small Groups

Wipf & Stock
An Imprint of Wipf and Stock Publishers
199 W. 8th Ave., Suite 3
Eugene, OR 97401

www.wipfandstock.com

PAPERBACK ISBN: 978-1-4982-9427-0
HARDCOVER ISBN: 978-1-4982-9429-4
EBOOK ISBN: 978-1-4982-9428-7

Manufactured in the U.S.A. 08/19/16

I would like to dedicate this work first to my loving and supportive wife, Mariya, for her strong faith in the Lord that inspired me to keep studying, researching, and writing. Her gentle spirit, genuine hospitality, and loving service in the ministry have been a tremendous blessing. Thank you for being a powerful prayer partner and a strong support.

Also, I dedicate this book to our children, Levi and Leyla, who were so patient throughout the whole project. Their love, acceptance, joyfulness, and cheerfulness have filled our home with joy, meaning, and laughter.

Contents

Foreword

Matthew 28: 16–20 The Great Commission

> Then the eleven disciples went to Galilee, to the mountain where Jesus had told them to go. When they saw him, they worshiped him; but some doubted. Then Jesus came to them and said, "All authority in heaven and on earth has been given to me. Therefore go and make disciples of all nations, baptizing them in the name of the Father and of the Son and of the Holy Spirit, and teaching them to obey everything I have commanded you. And surely I am with you always, to the very end of the age." (NIV)

People are leaving the church in record numbers and most wonder if they will ever come back. The Barna Research group states that "Millennials are leaving the church. Nearly six in ten (59%) young people who grow up in Christian churches end up walking away, and the unchurched segment among Millennials has increased in the last decade from 44% to 52%, mirroring a larger cultural trend away from churchgoing in America."[1] Research suggest the main reason for disengaging from worship is that their faith simply does not seem to connect to their daily lives.

The church today seems to have lots of folks who like the idea of Jesus and even the church and we patriciate as long as nothing better comes along. We have watched worship attendance norms

1. "The Priorities, Challenges, and Trends in Youth Ministry."

slide to the lowest common denominator. I have been serving my current church for four years and just this Easter a couple said to me as the left worship, "You must be the new pastor here, we are regulars but this is the first time we have seen you." Wow so that was a stretch even in the gracious world for "regular attendance" to mean once every four years? I think we have missed something. How do we make passionate disciples that have integrated their faith? How do we disciple the next generation of Jesus followers? I have some core belief about discipleship: disciples love God, love self and love others. These are Jesus words from the Shema (Deuteronomy 6:4–9). Followers of Jesus keep growing, maturing, and experiencing the amazing love of God, self, and others. This is discipleship.

I grew up in the United Methodist Tradition of our Christian faith. As I look back at discipleship and what connected me to God, it wasn't the church classes, mission trips, youth groups, or thousands of worship services that I attended that connected me, although that all played a part. What connected me in a spiritual, life-giving relationship with God was my relationship with the leaders in those classes, worship services, youth groups, etc.

I grew up mentored by lay people, teachers, farmers, business leaders. I was mentored by pastors active and retired. These are the people that helped me to integrate the teaching of Jesus into my life. The scriptures are full of multiple styles of discipleship. What does effective discipleship look like? What if we trained and mentored our youth in a biblical, relational way? The Rev. Dr. Edward Marton explores the idea of mentoring as mature believers invest their life in the life of another. You will be challenged to rethink what discipleship means and what it looks like in your church and in your life.

Dr. Marton will take us through historical example of mentorship of John Nevins Andrews by James White. He will help us to journey in the biblical model of mentorship as we look at Elisha being mentored by Elijah. Dr. Marton shares a new view of mentoring that has impacted his life and that he practices with great success. Truthfully, while disciple-making might be a priority for you, is your process working? What happens when we make life long disciples? Not just students, but real Jesus followers that change the world?

Grace and peace,

Rev. Dr. Duane A. Anders
Boise First United Methodist Church
The Cathedral of the Rockies

Acknowledgments

FIRST AND FOREMOST I would like to acknowledge and thank my Lord and Savior, Jesus Christ for his love, grace, and faithfulness. I would like to thank my mentors, Duane Anders and Mike Slaughter for their support, encouragement, prayers, and expertise. Thank you also to my faculty consultant Joni Sancken for her time in brain storming, advice, and scholarly editing. Thanks to my professional associates, Raj Attiken and Jeba Moses, for their wisdom, knowledge, and advice in reviewing and editing the document. Thanks to my peer group, Angela Billingslea, Doris Ing, Vance Ross, Chris Schoolcraft, and Anthony Stone, for their friendship, support, prayers, and encouragement. Thanks to my Mansfield Seventh-day Adventist Church context associates, Alice Grove, Patti Clayburn, Larry Clayburn, Rhonda Riles, Holbrook Riles, for their support, suggestions, and feedback. Thanks to my brothers for their support and prayers. Much appreciation and thanks to my parents: for my mother for her prayers, support, and encouragement; and to my father, who has fallen asleep in Jesus after battling lung cancer in 2010. He was the first mentor in my life, teaching me a strong work ethic and mentoring me in walking with the Lord. Though he lost the battle with cancer, he died in Christ, and has overcome. See you in the resurrection!

Last but not least, I thank my wife, Mariya, for her wonderful and loving support, always inspiring me to do my best, praying for me and with me throughout this project, and to my children, Levi and Leyla, for their patience, support, and cheerfulness.

Introduction

THE QUESTION LIES HOW could a congregation release and empower young people for ministry and disciples for service. The book looks at the development of mentoring and discipleship through small groups. In this book a distinction is made between mentoring and discipleship. Potential leaders are mentored to lead future small groups, while all small group members are to be discipled to follow Christ and to serve with Christ in the community.

Chapter One, "Mentors in the Life of a Mentee," defines the model of ministry, looks at mentors in my own spiritual journey.

Chapter Two, "Elijah's Effective Mentoring," describes the Old Testament mentoring of Elisha by Elijah.

Chapter Three, "Jesus, the Greatest Mentor," describes the New Testament mentoring of Peter by Jesus.

Chapter Four, "Mentoring in Early Seventh-day Adventism," describes the mentoring of John Nevins Andrews by James White in early Seventh-day Adventism. While the word itself "mentor" does not date back to the mid 1800s, the concept of mentoring is described.

Chapter Five, "Mentoring by the Design of the Holy Spirit," describes the role of the Holy Spirit in discipleship and mentoring. This section looks at the implications of pneumatology in Christology, soteriology, and ecclesiology, as they are interwoven with mentoring and discipleship.

Chapter Six, "College Campuses and Mentoring," the contemporary perspective looks at mentoring associated with college campuses, new students being mentored by more experienced students.

Chapter Seven, "Application and Mentoring," describes how mentoring was instituted through a project in the Mansfield Seventh-day Adventist Church through missional small groups.

The expected results are to create small groups in the Mansfield Seventh-day Adventist Church based on passions and gifts. The small groups would be a place of mentoring and discipleship while serving in the community. This way the church would be a place of mentoring for leadership and a place of discipleship for all members involved in small groups. The gospel would be taught in the community in tangible ways through the small groups using their gifts and passions.

Chapter Eight, "Mentoring in Youth Ministry," describes the practical application of mentoring in youth ministry in the Ohio Conference of Seventh-day Adventist.

Chapter 1

Mentors in the Life of a Mentee

Romania

THE MODEL OF MINISTRY considered in this book is mentoring and discipleship through small groups. There is a difference between mentoring and discipleship. A Christian disciple is a follower of Jesus Christ. Discipleship is a lifelong commitment to commune with Christ through prayer, meditation, and the study of the Scriptures. The life of a disciple includes other spiritual disciplines such as solitude, worship, simplicity, Sabbath rest, serving with Christ in the community, etc. On the other hand, a working definition for mentoring is, "Mentoring relationships are dynamic, reciprocal, personal relationships in which a more experienced person acts as a guide, role model, teacher, and sponsor of a less experienced person."[1] Therefore, while discipleship is a lifelong commitment, mentoring takes place for a period of time under a more experienced leader in order to develop into a successful leader.

Throughout my life, the theme of discipleship through mentoring was demonstrated over and over again. It seems the Lord was preparing me for ministry from a young age and did so through

1. Johnson, *The Elements of Mentoring*, xv.

spiritual mentors who were placed in my life providentially at different times. I was born August 5, 1978 in Turda, Romania. At that time, the country of Romania was under the dictatorship of Nicolae Ceausescu. It was a very challenging time for the country. As a child, I did not know all the struggles that people were going through, but I remember standing in line with my mom for hours to buy bread. Sometimes we stood in line for hours only to be turned away to have to return another day because everything was sold out.

There are very few memories of growing up in Romania, because in 1987, when I was eight years old we flew to start a new life in America. Yet some of the few memories of Romania include ice-skating across the street at a tennis court that would be flooded and the water frozen. Faithfully, the family also walked to church every Friday evening and Saturday morning.

The biggest memory of my early childhood revolves around the time my father escaped Romania. Mom and us three boys joined our father a few years later in Cleveland, Ohio. It all began when my father was arrested on charges that he had more flour, oil, and sugar in the pastry shop inventory, than was allowed by the government. He decided he had enough of communism and would flee the country. This decision and plan was carried out in the summer of 1985.

I was only six years old at the time and did not know any of the details, but do remember my father leaving and the house being ransacked by government authorities looking for clues to use and convict my father. We did not know for months whether our father was dead or alive, until one day a package arrived from Austria with some chocolate bars and a letter explaining that he was safe at an Austrian Refugee Camp. We were thankful to God for his loving protection over our father and for the privilege to communicate with him through letters.

Moving to United States of America

While our father was in Austria, he wanted his family to join him, but Austria made it a cumbersome process that would have taken about five years. The best option at the time was for him to try to get to the United States of America and within a year his family could join him. There was a Hungarian Seventh-day Adventist church in Westlake, Ohio and my father was able to contact the pastor of the church. The pastor sponsored him to come to America in 1988. The family arrived in Cleveland, Ohio, in the summer of 1989, to be reunited with our father.

What an experience to go through, to leave behind friends, uncles, aunts, cousins, a culture and to arrive in a new country, to make new friends, to learn a new language and a new culture. It was both an exciting and challenging experience even for an eight year-old boy. Since the Cleveland Ohio Hungarian Seventh-day Adventist church sponsored our family to come to America, we became very involved in church life. My two brothers were baptized by immersion in that church, and were involved in the orchestra and choir. Father and mother both became choir directors for the church choir and so the weekends revolved around church. The church had many active young people and a very involved youth and children's program. The pastor of the church included the children in the church service by beginning his sermons with a Biblical story and he would ask the children questions.

When I was eleven years old, an evangelist came to hold a series of evangelistic meetings at the church. When the appeal was made for baptism, together with my best friend, I made the decision to be baptized. Not only did I feel impressed by the Holy Spirit to be baptized, but also felt the call to full time ministry. Therefore I began planning for the ministry from the age of eleven. I did not know how or when God would bring to fruition the seed of the call to ministry, but I knew that it was God's call and it was my joy to respond. From the time of my baptism I also became involved in church. I would memorize poems and say them in church, sing songs, etc. During the week I would read my Bible, and witness to my school friends and teachers.

The family's life in Cleveland, Ohio lasted only three years. My father was enticed to move the family to Atlanta, Georgia because of a job offer from a friend. Father worked in construction, and Atlanta was booming with new buildings and houses. In Atlanta we attended the newly formed Romanian Seventh-day Adventist church. The family again became involved in the church.

A retired pastor from Romania was instrumental in starting up the Romanian church. I became close to him and he encouraged me to continue preparing for the ministry, even though I was only twelve years old. He would spend time playing tennis with me and quiz me on Bible trivia. He had a strong impact spiritually on my young life, preparing me to become a faithful servant of Christ. I learned from the retired pastor that mentoring is not done only at church but during social events, in places like a tennis court, a soccer field, or a basketball court.

In Atlanta, I started attending church school. The Romanian Seventh-day Adventist church met in a large American Seventh-day Adventist church that also operated a church school. It was a small school with approximately twenty to twenty five students from first through eighth grades. I really enjoyed the spiritual emphasis in the school. It was a great place for me to grow spiritually and to draw closer to Christ because Christ was uplifted.

During my last year at the church school tragedy struck our family. The family went to church to celebrate the New Year; 1991 was about to be history and 1992 was about to begin. Father was still at work, trying to finish some work on a house. He was planning to come to church later that evening. As we were playing in the church's gym with friends, we received a message that we needed to leave the party and go straight to the hospital. Father had an accident on the job and was at the hospital. He fell from the second floor scaffolding and landed on his head. The doctor at the hospital said that if he had hit his head a couple of inches higher, he would have died on the spot.

He broke one of his cheekbones and shattered the bones in his wrist. They put a plate in his face and had surgery on his hand. Since the family did not have health insurance, that put a heavy financial strain on the family. Father was the only source of income for the family, so my brothers tried to support the family financially for the next eight months.

After finishing eighth grade that year, the Lord opened up the opportunity for me to attend Atlanta Adventist Academy, a Seventh-day Adventist high school. While at Atlanta Adventist Academy, the Bible teacher, also had a spiritual impact upon my life. He would take time to pray with me, and his door was always open to answer Biblical questions or challenges that I was going through. The four years at the Academy was a time of spiritual growth, understanding spiritual things from an American culture instead of an Eastern European culture.

After finishing high school, my older brother convinced me to go with him for evangelism training at a small institution located in Hermosa, South Dakota called Mission College of Evangelism. We packed up a few things and started out for a road trip from Atlanta, Georgia to Hermosa, South Dakota.

Mission College of Evangelism was located in the beautiful Black Hills of South Dakota. The scenery was gorgeous; it really gave me the opportunity to come close to the God of nature and commune with the Creator of all things. Spiritually it was a powerful experience, to spend time with God in the Holy Scriptures, to have time to pray, and to learn how to witness effectively. It was exactly what I needed at the age of eighteen in order to grow close to God and to think about where God was leading me in His service.

The director of the school often encouraged me that "I can do all things through him who strengthens me."[2] One day the director asked if I would be interested in becoming a Bible instructor for a church. The proposition was scary since during the classes it was evident that giving Bible studies was my weakest point, but then I claimed Paul's words to the Corinthian believers, "And He

2. Philippians 4:13. Unless otherwise indicated, all Bible references in this thesis are to the New American Standard Bible (NASB).

said to me, 'My grace is sufficient for you, for power is perfected in weakness.' Most gladly, therefore, I will rather boast about my weaknesses, so that the power of Christ may dwell in me."[3]

I had a Romanian friend from Atlanta that also came to Mission College of Evangelism with us. He discouraged me and said that it could take from six to twelve months before any openings come up for a Bible instructor, so I should not get my hopes up. That was not the case, in fact, the following day I spoke on the phone with an associate pastor from a church in Wichita, Kansas.

The interview over the phone went well and they wanted me to drive to Wichita to see the church and to interview with the board members as well. After three weeks of training at Mission College of Evangelism, I went to Wichita, interviewed for the position and they hired me to be their Bible instructor. I was only paid a hundred and fifty dollars a month, but they gave me a place to stay and food to eat. I lived with the associate pastor and his lovely wife, O. J. and Millie Mills. They had been serving in the ministry for over fifty years by the time I went to live with them.

Living in their home for one and a half years was one of the best educations a young man could receive for the ministry. One of the first lessons I learned was the importance of spending time with the Lord in prayer, meditation, and Bible study. O.J.'s office was next to my bedroom. Early in the morning, around five o'clock, the office light would come on as O.J. in his early eighties, would commune with God.

At breakfast we would always discuss the Scriptures. Many times the topics would come to issues with which I as a young man was struggling. Could it be that the Holy Spirit communing with the elderly pastor inspired him to bring up topics that would benefit a young man entering the ministry? The answer was a definite "yes."

During the year and a half that I was doing Bible work in Wichita, I gained much experience in learning to talk to people, share the gospel, and teach the Bible. I would go into people's homes and study the Bible with them, as well as go on visits with

3. 2 Corinthians 12:9.

the senior pastor of the church. The senior pastor of the church, had a two-church district. When he was on vacation, he would allow me to preach at his smaller church that had an attendance of about ten to fifteen. That gave me the opportunity to practice my preaching skills. The pastor also had a huge impact in my life when it came to practical lessons in the ministry. He often invited me along for a hospital visit. He would then explain how hospital visits are to be conducted, what to talk about and what not to talk about, how short or long the visits should be, and so on. Other times he would invite me to an anointing service and explain how to anoint the sick. He would also invite me along on Bible studies and I would listen and learn as he gave Bible studies. For a young man in his late teens, such mentoring was heaven-sent.

Marriage and Ministry

When the year and a half came to an end, towards the end of 1998, I moved back to Atlanta, Georgia to sign up for Theology at Southern Adventist University. I was told to get my bachelor's degree in theology in order to enter the ministry, so I signed up to begin classes in the fall of 1999. Some events took place in the beginning of the year that changed all my plans for Southern Adventist University. First of all, I met my future wife at a youth retreat in February of 1999.

I was asked to be the youth leader for the Atlanta Romanian Seventh-day Adventist church. One of the things that I did was plan a retreat at Cohutta Springs, Georgia for young people. About thirty young people went to the retreat, and my future wife (I did not know it then), Mariya, happened to be one of them. We started talking at the retreat and found that we both wanted to serve the Lord in ministry. That providential appointment led to our marriage on December 5 of that same year.

We made a decision together, that instead of going to Southern Adventist University, we would go back to Mission College of Evangelism in Hermosa, South Dakota as a married couple.

I would take Bible classes and my bride would study health and massage therapy.

The year went by quickly with studying and living on campus. While there were many challenges, God blessed us tremendously and we were called at the end of the year to serve a small church as Bible instructors just outside of Grand Rapids, Michigan. We moved our few belongings from Hermosa to Grand Rapids. We had very few things, a car, some clothes, no bed to sleep on, no furniture to sit on and no table to dine on. The first gift we received from the kind members was an old television, so for the first few weeks we slept on the floor and ate on the floor next to the television.

Five months into serving as Bible instructors in Michigan, we received a phone call one Sabbath morning from the elder of the Hungarian Seventh-day Adventist church that I was baptized in at the age of eleven. The elder remembered that I felt called to the ministry and since their pastor just retired they were wondering what I was doing and if I wanted to interview for the position.

Mariya and I went to Ohio to preach and interview on Easter weekend 2001. The calling was for a two-church district, an English and a Hungarian church. The churches were located about fifteen miles apart and I would preach at both churches every weekend. Both the churches, Mariya, and I prayed about the call and we all felt that this was the Holy Spirit's leading, so we moved from Grand Rapids to Bay Village, a suburb of Cleveland, Ohio.

I was only twenty-two years old, scared and nervous, as well as enthusiastic about the opportunities that lay before us. I remember often falling on my knees that first year, asking the Lord for the anointing of the Holy Spirit. God blessed us in our first district as a pastoral couple. We served in that district for eight years and in those eight years, the English church went from an attendance of about thirty to ninety and in the Hungarian church from about sixty to about ninety as well.

Within eight years, our family also grew from two to four. Our firstborn son, Levi Nathanael entered our home on October 26, 2005 and Leyla Taylor graced our family with her presence on September 6, 2007. The children added joy, happiness and sleepless nights to our home. With our children growing, we desired to serve in an area that preferably had a church school for our children. Just as we were praying about God's will to move to a district with a church school, the pastor of the Mansfield Seventh-day Adventist Church accepted a ministry call to Florida.

Mariya and I put our names to fill the pastoral vacancy in Mansfield and were interviewed for the position in the summer of 2009. The church interviewed two other candidates, but they chose to hire us. We have been serving in this one church district in Mansfield, Ohio since the summer of 2009. We began our ministry making a covenant of support and accountability with the board members in our new church. We studied together the book *The Peace Maker* by Ken Sande. I wanted to lay a foundation of peace and peacemaking in the new district and to grow the church by having the leaders and members breathing grace and peace throughout Mansfield.

In 2010, I went through the most painful experience of my life. In February my father was diagnosed with Stage IV Lung Cancer. The doctor said he would pass away in about six months. The doctor was right, on September 6, 2010 my father lost the battle with lung cancer and passed away. It was the saddest experience of my life, to see cancer slowly destroy my strong father. Throughout my life, I have been blessed with godly role models, and I was privileged to have my father as one of those role models.

Father had a strong work ethic, he worked in construction and he would wake up early in the morning and work many hours till late at night in order to provide for his family. Though father worked hard, he always began the day with prayer, singing and studying Scripture. Because of his influence in my life, until this day I begin the day with prayer, singing, and studying Scripture, and I pray it is a habit that my children see, learn and will practice in their lives. I praise God for a father that modeled the importance of a daily devotional life and hard work and I look forward to the day when Jesus comes back and raises the righteous dead. I shall see my father again, enter the pearly gates of the New Jerusalem and sing praises to King Jesus for all eternity.

Today, as a husband, a father of two growing and healthy children, a pastor, a student, a son, and a citizen of Ohio, my greatest desire is to exemplify a life of discipleship in my home, in the church I am privileged to serve, and in the community that I live in. My passion is to mentor young people to be disciples of Jesus Christ in their homes, churches, and neighborhoods.

The disciples had Jesus as their only mentor, because he is Lord and the mentor of all mentors and disciples. God places many mentors in the lives of disciples today, for one person does not have all the qualifications to teach all the lessons in life; only the Lord Jesus Christ is able to do so. In my life, God has placed many mentors in my pathway. The first mentors in my life were my parents, my father and mother, and every father and mother ought to consider themselves as the first mentors of their children. But God had placed other spiritual mentors in my life that took me to the tennis court and played tennis with me, brought me to a table filled with delicious and appetizing food and shared meals with me, and invited me along to visit, anoint, and pray with people. Those experiences taught me many invaluable lessons, but the most important lesson of all was how mentoring takes place in the daily life.

There are numerous examples in the Bible of effective mentoring. In the following chapters we will look at two of those examples. Elijah's mentoring of Elisha and Jesus' mentoring of Peter. Mentoring has been a key component of my spiritual and leadership growth and you probably had individuals who were mentors in your life. Think about the individuals that have mentored you in life, in what ways have they blessed and enriched your life? Now think of the young people in your home, if you're a parent, the young people in your neighborhood or church that the Lord wants you to mentor, what are ways that you are able to be a mentor to young people? God has called you to be mentored and to be a mentor, ask the Holy Spirit to guide you as you follow Christ in mentoring others, including children, youth, and young adults.

Chapter 2

Elijah's Effective Mentoring

Similarities and Differences Between Mentoring and Discipling

MENTORING IS PRACTICED IN many areas of life, from the home life to the business world, and beyond. Experienced individuals develop relationships in order to train, guide, and teach inexperienced individuals in a certain profession and/or life experience they are proficient in. Mentoring then is not the same as discipling. Discipling is "helping new believers grow in Christ. A more mature believer helps a new believer grow in following Jesus."[1] Mentoring on the other hand is "empowering emerging leaders. A mature leader helps an emerging leader both clarify and implement God's call."[2] While mentoring and discipling are two different disciplines, they may at times overlap, when an emerging leader being mentored is also discipled as a follower of Christ. An example of this is Jesus' mentoring and discipling of Peter. We will explore Jesus and Peter in the following chapter, but purpose of this chapter is to demonstrate through biblical passages the significance of mentoring through the narratives of Elijah's mentoring of Elisha.

1. Crow, "Multiplying Jesus Mentors," 36, 90.

2. Ibid.

This narrative will highlight the connection between mentor and mentee, also considering that the mentees received and continued ministering in the "spirit" of their mentors.

This chapter will first focus on 2 Kings 4, looking at Elisha raising the Shunammite's son. As a background to the study, this chapter explores how Elisha became a mentee of Elijah (1 Kings 19:19–21). It looks at how Elisha received a double share of Elijah's spirit (2 Kings 2:1–18). Then it explores the similarities and differences between Elijah raising the son of the widow of Zarephath (1 Kings 17:17–24) and Elisha raising the Shunammite's son. Finally it will conclude that Elijah's mentoring and double sharing of his spirit was influential in Elisha's raising the Shunammite's son.

Elisha Meets Elijah

Elisha was the successor of Elijah as the prophet of God of Israel. It was the Lord who told Elijah to anoint Elisha as his successor. After the showdown between Elijah and the priests of Baal on Mount Carmel, Elijah had all the priests of Baal killed (see 1 Kings 18:40). Then Elijah became afraid when he heard the news that Jezebel planned to kill him (see 1 Kings 19:1–3). He fled from Jezreel and ended up at Horeb where God told him to anoint "Hazael as king over Aram" (1 Kings 19:15), "Jehu the son of Nimshi you shall anoint king over Israel" (1 Kings 19:16), and "Elisha son of Shaphat of Abel-meholah you shall anoint as prophet in your place" (1 Kings 19:17).

Elijah went to Elisha, who was plowing with twelve yoke of oxen and threw his mantle over Elisha. Walter Brueggemann notes that the by this action "Elisha is recruited as the follower and successor of Elijah."[3] Elisha understood the call of Elijah, for he said to him, "Please let me kiss my father and my mother, then I will follow you" (1 Kings 19:20). Elisha then "took the pair of oxen and sacrificed them and boiled their flesh with the implements of the oxen, and gave it to the people and they ate. Then he arose and

3. Brueggemann, *1 & 2 Kings*, 239.

followed Elijah and ministered to him." (1 Kings 19:21). August Konkel writes that there is a reason why Elisha burned the yoke of the oxen. "The burning of the yoke of the oxen signifies a complete break with the past. From that time on Elisha becomes the protégé of Elijah."[4]

According to Brueggemann, when Elisha left everything and followed Elijah, he became "fully Elijah's recruit and, by implication Yahweh's man."[5] Peter Leithart states, that Elisha "becomes an apprentice to Elijah, in order to become like his master."[6] And Volkmar Fritz notes that from that moment on, Elisha's "relationship to Elijah is thought of as a personal discipleship that results in succession, just as the 'servant' Joshua had become the successor to Moses (see Exod 24:13; 33:1; Num 11:28; Josh 1:1)."[7] To go a step further from Fritz, it was not only personal discipleship, but also mentoring that took place between Elijah and Elisha. Therefore, before Elijah's ascension to heaven he spent time mentoring Elisha so that Elisha would continue the ministry that Elijah had been doing.

Not only did Elisha become Elijah's protégé, but he also asked for and received a double portion of his spirit. As Elijah and Elisha were walking from Jericho to the Jordan River, with his mantle Elijah parted the river so they could walk across on dry ground. Then he asked Elisha, "Ask what I shall do for you before I am taken from you" (2 Kings 2:9). Elisha answered, "Please, let a double portion of your spirit be upon me" (2 Kings 2:9). Elijah responded, "You have asked a hard thing. *Nevertheless*, if you see me when I am taken from you, it shall be so for you; but if not, it shall not be so" (2 Kings 2:10).

Regarding Elisha's request for a double portion, "the Hebrew phrase employed is the same as that in Deut 21:17, denoting the proportion of a father's property that was to be given to the eldest

4. Konkel, *1 & 2 Kings*, 304.

5. Brueggemann, *1 & 2 Kings*, 239.

6. Leithart, *1 & 2 Kings*, 143.

7. Fritz, *1 & 2 Kings*, 201.

son."[8] Elisha then is asking to be like Elijah's eldest son. "What he was asking for was an acknowledgment of a spiritual birthright, that he might be regarded as the first-born spiritual son of the elder prophet, and that he might thus be enabled to continue the work begun by Elijah."[9] Elijah's response to Elisha's request indicated that this was a hard request to grant and would be granted if he saw Elijah's ascension.

Elisha did see the ascension of Elijah and as Elijah ascended to heaven in a whirlwind, his mantle fell to the ground. He picked up the mantle of Elijah, went back to the Jordan River and parted it the way Elijah just did earlier. "Now when the sons of the prophets who *were* at Jericho opposite *him* [Elisha] saw him, they said, 'The spirit of Elijah rests on Elisha'" (2 Kings 2:15). Elisha received what he requested, a double share of Elijah's spirit. Two chapters after this event, in 2 Kings 4, is a demonstration, not only of how effective Elijah's mentoring was in the life and ministry of Elisha but also how the double portion of Elijah's spirit rested upon Elisha.

Elisha and the Shunammite Woman

The story of the raising of the Shunammite's son is the second of four stories recorded in 2 Kings 4. In these four stories, the prophet Elisha performed five miracles. In the first miracle Elisha helped a poor widow pay off her debt in order to keep her children from being taken by the creditors. In the second story, Elisha performed a double miracle for a family that blessed him with great hospitality by giving him accommodations during his travels. In the third miracle Elisha fixed a pot of stew that was poisonous by adding some flour to the stew. And in the fourth miracle Elisha multiplied twenty barley loaves in order to feed a hundred people.

These four stories are not random selections juxtaposed to each other. "These are stories about the people and represent those who are in need. Spotlighting the plight of individuals or small

8. Nichol, "Joshua to 2 Kings," 851.

9. Ibid., 851, 952.

groups rather than the whole amorphous Israel, they convey a more personal sense of the plight of the peasants."[10] It is true that in all four stories each one has some need and those needs are different, but in the case of the Shunammite woman, she does not represent the "plight of the peasants," for she was not poor, but wealthy. These stories also have commonality with Elisha's mentor Elijah. "The miracles of these stories have counterparts in the activities of Elijah. The multiplication of oil (vv. 4–5) and of bread (vv. 43–44) and the revival of a widow's son (vv. 33–35) are similar to the provisions of Elijah for the widow of Zarephath (1 Kings 17:14–16, 20–22). Elisha is again shown to be the worthy successor of Elijah."[11]

Returning to the second story in 2 Kings 4, where Elisha blessed a family with a double miracle because of their hospitality, the story is shared in two parts. The first part is the gift of a baby boy to the Shunammite family and the second part is the raising of the Shunammite boy. The first part of the story explains how Elisha comes to know the Shunammite family, has the first miracle, and lays the foundation for the second miracle, in the second part of the story.

> Now there came a day when Elisha passed over to Shunem, where there was a prominent woman, and she persuaded him to eat food. And so it was, as often as he passed by, he turned in there to eat food. She said to her husband, "Behold now, I perceive that this is a holy man of God passing by us continually. Please, let us make a little walled upper chamber and let us set a bed for him there, and a table and a chair and a lamp-stand; and it shall be, when he comes to us, *that* he can turn in there." One day he came there and turned in to the upper chamber and rested. Then he said to Gehazi his servant, "Call this Shunammite." And when he had called her, she stood before him. He said to him, "Say now to her, 'Behold, you have been careful for us with all this care; what can I do for you? Would you be spoken for to the

10. Hens-Piazza, *1–2 Kings*, 249.

11. Konkel, *1 & 2 Kings*, 417.

> king or to the captain of the army?'" And she answered, "I live among my own people." So he said, "What then is to be done for her?" And Gehazi answered, "Truly she has no son and her husband is old." He said, "Call her." When he had called her, she stood in the doorway. Then he said, "At this season next year you will embrace a son." And she said, "No, my lord, O man of God, do not lie to your maidservant." The woman conceived and bore a son at that season the next year, as Elisha had said to her.[12]

As Elisha was passing through Shunem, a prominent and wealthy Shunammite woman urged and persuaded Elisha to stop in her home for a meal. This became a custom for Elisha, whenever he would travel through, he would stop in for a meal. Again, the Shunammite woman takes the initiative to ask her husband to build a room on the roof for Elisha so that whenever he came by, he would not only have a meal, but a place of rest. Sure enough, a walled chamber was built upon the roof for Elisha with a bed, a table, a chair, and a lamp.

In ancient Israel, roofs were flat and they were used in a similar manner that North Americans use their basement. Since roofs were so useful in Old Testament times, a law was given in Deuteronomy 22:8 to make a parapet on the roof so that people would not fall to their death. When the spies were in Jericho, Rahab hid them on her roof in the stalks of flax—David also was walking on the top of his roof when he saw Bathsheba bathing (2 Samuel 11:2). And it was not uncommon to have guests staying on the roof while visiting for a longer period of time. Such was the case with Saul when he visited Samuel in 1 Samuel 9:25, 26. Significantly for this study, Elijah also stayed on the roof when visiting the widow of Zarephath in 1 Kings 17:19.[13]

Elisha wished to show his appreciation to the woman for her hospitality and offered to do something for her in return. She did not want anything, but Gehazi, Elisha's servant, informed him that she was childless and without hope of having a child because

12. 2 Kings 4:8–17.

13. Provan, *1 & 2 Kings*, 3:129.

her husband was old. Brueggemann reminds of the fact that "it is impossible to overestimate the cruciality of a son in that ancient, patriarchal world. A son guaranteed economic surety in time to come, and lack of a son was a social stigma to a woman."[14] Volkmar goes even further to point out that giving birth to a son "also meant the greatest fulfillment in the life of a woman."[15] For her to have a son then would have been one of the greatest blessings possible.

Yet when Elisha promised a son, the Shunammite woman did not sound ecstatic in her response. No reason is given for her less-than-enthusiastic response; was it because she had tried to have a child but was unable to get pregnant? Or was she surprised, delighted, but still uncertain of the prophet's words? But whatever the reason, she does have a son and with the joy of a little baby, the first part of the story ends.

The second part of the story begins with a crisis. But just as the first part ended with the woman receiving the miracle of a baby boy, the second part finishes with another miracle, this time the woman receiving back her boy from death.

> When the child was grown, the day came that he went out to his father to the reapers. He said to his father, "My head, my head." And he said to his servant, "Carry him to his mother." When he had taken him and brought him to his mother, he sat on her lap until noon, and *then* died . . . When Elisha came into the house, behold the lad was dead and laid on his bed. So he entered and shut the door behind them both and prayed to the Lord. And he went up and lay on the child, and put his mouth on his mouth and his eyes on his eyes and his hands on his hands, and he stretched himself on him; and the flesh of the child became warm. Then he returned and walked in the house once back and forth, and went up and stretched himself on him; and the lad sneezed seven times and the lad opened his eyes. He called Gehazi and said, "Call this Shunammite." So he called her. And when she came in to him, he said, "Take up your son." Then she went in and

14. Brueggemann, *1 & 2 Kings*, 322.

15. Fritz, *1 & 2 Kings*, 251.

> fell at his feet and bowed herself to the ground, and she took up her son and went out.[16]

The second part of the story began with the Shunammite woman again taking the initiative. This time she asked her husband for a servant and a donkey to go see Elisha. "Shunem is only about fifteen miles from the traditional location of Elijah's sacrifice (*Deir al-Mahraq*), and the name of the hill at Shunem (Moreh) makes it likely there is a prophetic community located there where Elisha can receive hospitality."[17] Though Elisha sent Gehazi to go and place his staff on the boy, the woman does not leave with Gehazi, but she pleaded with Elisha to go with her. Elisha goes with her and he raised the boy back to life in a fashion similar to how Elijah raised the son of the widow of Zarephath in 1 Kings 17:17–24.

Similarities and Differences

Similarities and differences can be seen in this story between Elisha and his mentor Elijah. Starting with the contrasts, in Elijah's case, he was the one that initiated the conversation with the widow of Zarephath, he asked for food from her. But with Elisha, it was the Shunammite that urged him to come and stay for a meal. While Elisha was distant towards the woman by talking to her through Gehazi, Elijah spoke directly to the widow of Zarephath. When the son of the widow of Zarephath died, Elijah was present and responded quickly. Yet when the son of the Shunammite died, Elisha was not only absent but also sent Gehazi in response, and the Shunammite had to persuade him to personally come and help her in the dire emergency of her son's death. Elijah's prayer is recorded while Elisha's prayer is not. And Elijah stretched out over the body three times while Elisha lay upon the boy twice. In Elijah's narrative the widow responded with words to the raising of her son,

16. 2 Kings 4:18–20, 32–37.

17. Konkel, *1 & 2 Kings*, 418, 419.

while in Elisha's narrative the woman responded with her actions by bowing at his feet.[18]

On the other hand "the Midrash says Elijah did eight miracles and Elisha sixteen. Elisha's miracles not only double Elijah's but seem to parallel and multiply them in their themes, elements and language."[19] Perhaps the reason why twice as many miracles are recorded for Elisha is because he asked for a double share of Elijah's spirit. Another reason given for the duplicate amount of miracles is for Elisha to be recognized as a prophet in his own right. "Elisha duplicates some miracles performed by his mentor for a number of reasons. He wishes to honor Elijah's memory, he seeks to realize his own power, and he wants to be seen by others as a prophet of God in his own right."[20]

This leads to the fact that there are not only some differences within the stories but also between the prophetic styles of Elijah and Elisha. "Elisha is more lenient and humane with enemy soldiers than Elijah was under similar circumstances. Elisha allows the Aramean soldiers to return to their land in safety, whereas Elijah lets fire consume those who sought to apprehend him (II Kgs. 6:21–23; 2 Kgs. 1:9–12)."[21]

There are further differences between Elijah and Elisha to the style of their prophetic ministry.

> The work of Elisha as a prophet was in some respects very different from that of Elijah. To Elijah had been committed messages of condemnation and judgment; his was the voice of fearless reproof, calling king and people to turn from their evil ways. Elisha's was a more peaceful mission; his it was to build up and strengthen the work that Elijah had begun; to teach the people the way of the Lord.[22]

18. Shields, "Subverting a Man of God," 58, 59–69.
19. Levine, "Twice as Much of Your Spirit," 25.
20. Zucker, "Elijah and Elisha," 20.
21. Ibid., 21.
22. White, *Prophets and Kings*, 235.

> Elijah often acts alone, even without attendants. By contrast, Elisha is often associated with a company of prophets and/or is attended by a named servant, Gehazi. Elisha seems to live in a community of prophets. Elijah is very self-reliant. With one exception, dispatching his servant to look west for a sign of rain, Elijah performs his prophetic acts alone. By contrast, Elisha often delegates someone to bring the prophetic message (1 Kgs. 18:43–44; II Kgs. 4:43; 5:8, 10; 9:1–3).[23]

"In terms of their physical appearance, the prophets also differ: Elijah is described as being hairy, while Elisha is bald (II Kgs. 1:8; 2:23)."[24] As well as in terms of their pre-prophetic history, they are widely different. "Whereas the Bible is silent about Elijah's pre-prophetic history, not even mentioning his father's name, the text indicates that Elisha ben Shaphat came from a wealthy family."[25] David Zucker concludes the differences by writing: "Although Elisha patterned certain of his miraculous acts after those of his mentor Elijah, in many ways their prophetic styles differed. Each prophet was distinctive, bringing a special message and approach to his role."[26]

There are numerous and definite similarities between Elijah and Elisha's ministries. Elijah multiplied oil and meal for the widow of Zarephath in order for her to make bread (1 Kings 17:15, 16). Elisha also multiplied oil for a widow in 2 Kings 4:1–7 that she may pay off her debt and later multiplied bread in 2 Kings 4:42–44 that one hundred people may be fed.[27]

The miracles happened both for the Shunammite and for the widow of Zarephath because they provided a room for the prophets of God. And in both instances the room provided was a chamber upon the roof. Both in Elijah and Elisha's cases there is a preliminary miracle before they raised the boys, for Elijah the

23. Zucker, "Elijah and Elisha," 21.

24. Ibid.

25. Ibid.

26. Ibid., 22.

27. Brueggemann, *1 & 2 Kings*, 322.

preliminary miracle was the multiplication of oil and meal and for Elisha it was the miracle of the boy in the first place.[28] "Like the woman at Zarephath, who held Elijah responsible for the death of her son (1 Kings 17:18), the woman from Shunem feels that there is something sinister about this man of God; he has deceived her (2 Kings 4:28)."[29]

In raising the boy, Elisha prayed to the Lord and then lay upon the child (2 Kings 4:34, 35), as did Elijah, who also prayed and lay upon the child. As about the similarities in how Elijah and Elisha prayed: "In 1 Kgs 18.42 Elijah bows low to pray for rain as does Elisha over the boy to bring him life (2 Kgs 4.34)."[30] Both sons were given twice in a sense, for if it would not have been for the presence of Elijah in the life of the widow, her boy and the widow would have died after they ate their last meal. And if it had not been for the presence of Elisha in the home of the Shunammite, she would not have had her son in the first place. And the last similarity between the ministries of Elisha and Elijah is the return of the raised sons to their mothers. "Elisha returns the son, now alive, to the mother with the same terseness as Elijah's parallel in 1 Kings 17:23."[31]

All these similarities, not only in this story but also between the narratives of Elijah and Elisha, suggest that Elijah spent time mentoring Elisha for his ministry and that Elisha also received a double share of Elijah's spirit. Therefore, while the differences reveal that Elijah and Elisha had different prophetic styles and had their own approach to service, the similarities show that mentoring is one effective way to prepare someone for serving the Lord.

28. Ibid.

29. Konkel, *1 & 2 Kings*, 415.

30. Levine, "Twice as Much of Your Spirit," 34.

31. Brueggemann, *1 & 2 Kings*, 324.

Chapter 3

Jesus, the Greatest Mentor

Jesus Chooses Disciples to Mentor

THIS CHAPTER WILL FOCUS on the effective mentoring of Jesus in the life of Peter. The chapter will focus on Acts 9, looking at Peter raising Tabitah as an example of how Peter learned to minister and serve from his Lord and Savior, Jesus Christ, who also mentored him in service. As a background to the study, we will also explore Peter's call to discipleship by Jesus. It will look at the outpouring of the Holy Spirit upon the disciples on the day of Pentecost (Acts 2). It will show how Peter's raising of Tabitha had similarities to Jesus' raising of the young girl (Luke 8:40–56). It will show how Jesus' mentoring of Peter was effective and influential in Peter raising Tabitha. Through the chosen stories of Elisha and Peter, it will be shown how helpful the experience of mentoring was in their ministries.

Jesus also chose disciples to mentor in the ministry, to continue the work after his death, resurrection, and ascension to heaven. Luke 5:1–11 provides the story of four individuals who were asked by Jesus to become his disciples. One individual that came to center stage of Christ's call was Peter. "Simon Peter is the best known of the apostles. He is mentioned 182 times in the New

Testament, more often than all the others added together. In contrast John's name appears 50 times, James' 21, and the remaining nine less frequently."[1] In fact in every list of the twelve disciples, Peter's name is mentioned first (Matthew 10:2–4; Mark 3:16–19; Luke 6:13–16; Acts 1:13).[2] According to William Barclay, Peter was the best leader from the disciples chosen by Jesus.[3] MacArthur states about Peter that he "stands out as the leader and spokesman for the whole company of twelve."[4] Peter was the name given to him by Jesus (John 1:42); his name was Simon, or Simeon in its Gentile form.[5]

From Luke's narrative, Peter lived in Capernaum and he was a fisherman. In Luke 5:3 Jesus got into Peter's boat and began teaching the crowd that came out to hear him. This was not the first encounter of Peter with Jesus. In Luke 4:38, 39 Jesus was a guest at Peter's home and healed his mother-in-law of a high fever. Jesus teaching the crowd from Peter's boat then was at least a second encounter with Jesus. As Jesus taught, Peter and the crowd listen. After Jesus was done teaching, he directed Peter to "put out into the deep water and let down your nets for a catch" (Luke 5:4). Peter protested, "Master, we worked hard all night and caught nothing, but I will do as You say and let down the nets" (Luke 5:5). When they let down their nets, "they enclosed a great quantity of fish, and their nets *began* to break" (Luke 5:6). Peter realizing what just happened, fell down at the feet of Jesus, exclaiming, "Go away from me, Lord, for I am a sinful man!" (Luke 5:8). Rather than leaving Peter, Jesus invited him to become one of his disciples, "do not fear, from now on you will be catching people" (Luke 5:10, NRSV). Peter responded to Jesus' invitation and with the others called by Jesus, "when they brought their boats to land, they left everything and followed him" (Luke 5:11).

Regarding the call of Peter's discipleship, Joel B. Green writes;

1. Hardinge, *Ambassadors*, 41.
2. MacArthur, *Twelve Ordinary Men*, 29.
3. Barclay, *The Master's Men*, 15.
4. MacArthur, *Twelve Ordinary Men*, 29.
5. Barclay, *The Master's Men*, 15, 16.

> Luke's version also makes discipleship more of a process than an immediate and sudden change . . . First, he observes Jesus healing his mother-in-law and eats with him. Next, he does Jesus a favor and listens to him teach. Next, although he doubts Jesus knows anything about fishing, he obeys the command to fish—something he already knows how to do—and experiences the miracle in the context of his own livelihood. Only then is he ready to repent and to launch out into the truly deep waters of full-time discipleship.[6]

Robert Coleman makes the case that Christ's evangelistic strategy was to train individuals that would impact the world after his departure. "It all started by Jesus calling a few men to follow him. This revealed immediately the direction his evangelistic strategy would take . . . Men [sic] were to be his method of winning the world to God."[7] According to Coleman, the criteria that Jesus used choose those to be part of his small group included those who were teachable, honest, willing to confess their need, and had big hearts.[8] In order for the church to make in impact in the community and in the world, there has to be time for the training and mentoring of leaders. "This will require more concentration of time and talents on fewer people in the church while not neglecting the passion for the world."[9] We are then to follow in the footsteps of Jesus, using the method of mentoring and discipleship in order to successfully impact the world.

In his article, Crow clarifies that Jesus did not only call the twelve to discipleship but also to mentoring.[10] Based upon Christ's call of the twelve as recorded in Mark 3:13–15 and Luke 6:12–13, Crow mentions eight dynamics to the process of selecting the twelve to mentor. First, there was a large group of people that followed Jesus, Crow says that this was "widespread, follower-initiated

6. Green, *The Gospel of Luke*, 235.

7. Coleman, *The Master Plan of Evangelism*, 27.

8. Ibid., 29.

9. Ibid., 36.

10. Crow, "Multiplying Jesus Mentors," 36.

discipleship."[11] Second, Jesus spends an entire night in prayer, "he sought God diligently about who His mentorees should be . . . He sought a Spirit-directed decision."[12]

The third dynamic of Jesus' selection process in his mentoring methodology was personal affinity. "Personal affinity, filtered by prayer, played a significant part in Jesus' choice of His mentorees."[13] Fourth, Jesus initiated the call to mentoring, "when day came, He called His disciples to Him and chose twelve of them" (Luke 6:13). Fifth, the disciples accepted the invitation of Jesus; they were not forced into a mentor/mentee relationship. Sixth, as the twelve responded to the call of mentorship, "Jesus formalized this mentoring relationship. Specific individuals were selected and given specific roles and responsibilities."[14] Seventh, "an intensified relational network was the immediate context of mentoring."[15] Jesus took the disciples everywhere with him, it seems that he is rarely alone from this point forward. And last part of the selection process was to send them out at times to practice what he has taught them. "Jesus appointed them 'to be sent out' to preach and exorcise demons. At times He sent them out in twos to minister apart from him. At other times they served beside him (e.g., in feeding the 5,000). Active ministry responsibility, at minimum in pairs, was the larger context for mentoring."[16] Through Crow's eight dynamics of Christ's selection process, we could conclude that Christ called the disciples to a journey of mentorship.

Crow also mentions eight characteristics of Christ's mentoring methodology with Peter and the other eleven:

> *He Invested More in the Committed Few than in the Curious Many:* Jesus seemed to deliberately weed out sensation-seekers, curious only in signs and wonders.

11. Ibid., 91.
12. Ibid.
13. Ibid.
14. Ibid.
15. Ibid.
16. Ibid.

He wanted commitment, those who had left all to follow Him.

He Modeled Holistically: the Twelve observed Jesus in all kinds of situations: when He was tired, angry and praying; when He debated opponents and confronted political powers; when He comforted the grieving and when He grieved Himself; when He preached, healed sickness and exorcised demons; when He ate and even when He slept. Jesus modeled life and ministry holistically, not selectively (e.g., lecture only).

He Inspired Small Group Interaction: Jesus formed the Twelve into a cohesive whole, who served and interacted with Him *and* with each other. Not only did they ask Him questions, they had discussions among themselves. While ministry was the larger context for Jesus' mentoring program, small group interaction—with Jesus and with each other—was the immediate context.

He Mentored One-on-One: Jesus confronted the Samaritan woman's lifestyle and addressed Thomas's doubts. He questioned Nicodemus and taught Mary. He restored Peter and challenged John. Jesus mentored in ways tailored to each individual.

He Privately Explained Public Ministry: the disciples asked Jesus questions about his preaching and received further explanation in private settings. These discussions were characterized, not by prepared lessons, but by spontaneous question-and-answer.

He Gave Them Ministry Assignments: Jesus sent the Twelve out to preach, exorcise demons and heal disease, thus multiplying His ministry to the needy. He taught them how to handle money, receptivity and rejection. He modeled ministry, sent them to minister—always in pairs—and involved them actively in His own ministry.

He Envisioned Multiplication: in compassion for people suffering under spiritual tyranny, Jesus urged prayer for more shepherd-laborers. He commanded the disciples to make disciples who would make disciples who would

> make disciples. Jesus envisioned leadership reproducibility and multiplication.
>
> *He Spent Much Time with Them:* Jesus rarely had "alone time," except in prayer. He was not an absentee mentor. He spent much informal time with the disciples: walking, sitting in houses or in boats, feasting and ministering. Just as Jesus called them to be *"with him"* (Mk. 3:14), He also took significant time to be *"with them"* (Lk. 6:17; Mt. 26:36; Lk. 24:14; Jn. 3:22; 4:39; 14:23). Jesus was a "very present" mentor.[17]

We could add one more characteristic to Crow's eight, and that is the role of the Holy Spirit in Christ mentoring Peter and the eleven. For Peter not only left all and became a disciple of Jesus, but according to Acts, he also experienced the outpouring of the Holy Spirit. Jesus, who was born by the Holy Spirit (Luke 1:35), full of the Holy Spirit (Luke 4:1), promised the outpouring of the Holy Spirit upon his disciples in Acts 1:8, "But you will receive power when the Holy Spirit has come upon you; and you shall be My witnesses both in Jerusalem, and in all Judea and Samaria, and even to the remotest part of the earth." This promise was fulfilled in Acts 2:1–4:

> When the day of Pentecost had come, they were all together in one place. And suddenly there came from heaven a noise like a violent rushing wind, and it filled the whole house where they were sitting. And there appeared to them tongues as of fire distributing themselves, and they rested on each one of them. And they were all filled with the Holy Spirit and began to speak with other tongues, as the Spirit was giving them utterance.[18]

Peter again took center stage in Acts 2 and addressed the crowd. In his address he proclaimed that Jesus was resurrected and "exalted to the right hand of God, and having received from the Father the promise of the Holy Spirit, He has poured forth this which you both see and hear" (Acts 2:33). Peter not only followed

17. Ibid., 92.

18. Acts 2:1–4.

Jesus as a disciple and was mentored by Christ, but also received the Spirit from Jesus that was present in the life of Jesus.

Peter and Tabitha

In the story of Peter raising Tabitha, we see how effective Jesus' discipleship and mentorship, and the presence of the Holy Spirit was in his life.

> Now in Joppa there was a disciple whose name was Tabitha, which in Greek is Dorcas. She was devoted to good works and acts of charity. At that time she became ill and died. When they had washed her, they laid her in a room upstairs. Since Lydda was near Joppa, the disciples, who heard that Peter was there, sent two men to him with the request, "Please come to us without delay." So Peter got up and went with them; and when he arrived, they took him to the room upstairs. All the widows stood beside him, weeping and showing tunics and other clothing that Dorcas had made while she was with them. Peter put all of them outside, and then he knelt down and prayed. He turned to the body and said, "Tabitha, get up." Then she opened her eyes, and seeing Peter, she sat up. He gave her his hand and helped her up. Then calling the saints and widows, he showed her to be alive. This became known throughout Joppa, and many believed in the Lord. Meanwhile he stayed in Joppa for some time with a certain Simon, a tanner.[19]

This story is the second of three stories about Peter that are recorded in the middle portion of the book of Acts. The first story, the healing of Aeneas is the shortest of the three stories, with only four verses. In the second story, Peter raised Tabitha who died; this passage is recorded in eight verses. And the last story is the conversion of Cornelius and it is the longest of the three stories with forty-eight verses.

Each succeeding story gives more details than the previous story. Each story builds on the previous one, while at the same

19. Acts 9:36–43, NRSV.

time preparing for the following story, with a crescendo of the conversion of Cornelius and his household. "The story of Tabitha is a hinge between the healing of Aeneas, which shows that Peter exercised a similar ministry both within and beyond Jerusalem (3:1–10), and the elaborately narrated conversion of Cornelius."[20]

From this story we can gather that there were Jesus believers in Joppa, for one of the disciples named Tabitha became sick and died. It is interesting to note that, "this is the only time in the New Testament that the feminine form of the Greek word 'disciple' is found."[21] She was a very faithful, generous, and hard-working disciple, "devoted to good works and acts of charity" (Acts 9:36).

There was probably closeness between the Christian group of Lydda and that of Joppa. The Christian group heard that Peter was in Lydda, probably they heard how he healed Aeneas and when Tabitha passed away they requested Peter to quickly track the ten miles northwest to Joppa.[22] Why the haste for Peter to come quickly since Tabitha was dead already? No reason is given for the hurry, but Peter responded by going to Joppa and when he arrived, he went into the upper room and found that there were weeping widows waiting to show him all the good works that Tabitha had done. Peter asked everyone to step outside, so he remained alone in the room with Tabitha's dead body. He knelt down and prayed, afterwards said to Tabitha, "Tabitha, get up." She responded by opening her eyes and sitting up.

There are distinct similarities between Peter raising Tabitha and Jesus raising the daughter of Jairus. Jairus appealed to Jesus to come heal his daughter who was dying (Luke 8:41), and the Christian group at Joppa begged Peter to come because Tabitha had died (Acts 9:38). When Jesus arrived at Jairus' house, he was met with people weeping the young girl's death (Luke 8:52), and when Peter arrives to Joppa, he was met in the upper room with weeping widows (Acts 9:39).

20. Pervo, *Acts,* Hermeneia, 253, 254.

21. Rius-Camps, *The Message of Acts in Codex Bezae,* 211–212.

22. Ibid., 213, 214.

Jesus asked everyone to leave the room except her mother, father and James, John, and Peter before the miracle of raising the young girl (Luke 8:51). Peter also asked everyone to step outside when he raised Tabitha (Acts 9:40). Jesus spoke to the young girl as he was about to raise her by saying "child, get up!" (Luke 8:54) and Peter also spoke to Tabitha as he was about to raise her by saying "Tabitha, get up" (Acts 9:40).

Just as the young girl responded to Jesus, so Tabitha responded to Peter. Like Jesus took the young girl by the hand as he was raising her (Luke 8:54), Peter took Tabitha by the hand, but only after she was raised (Acts 9:41). After Jesus spoke the words and took her hand, the young girl got up (Luke 8:55), Tabitha also responded to Peter's words and sat up (Acts 9:40).

There are also similarities between Peter raising Tabitha and how Elijah raised the widow's son and how Elisha raised the Shunammite's son. Bradley Chance notes some of these similarities:

> Tabitha's friends place her in an upper room (*hyproio*), v. 37. Elijah places the dead child in an upper room (*hyproon*), 1 Kgs 17:17, 23. Peter removes the mourners from the room, v. 40a . . . Both Elijah and Elisha perform their miracles of resuscitation in private (1 Kgs 17;18; 2 Kgs 4:32). Peter prays, v. 40b. Elijah "cried out" to God (1 Kgs 17:20–21); Elisha "prayed to the Lord" (2 Kgs 4:33). Tabitha "opened her eyes," v. 40c. The child raised by Elisha "opened his eyes" (2 Kgs 4:35). Peter presented Tabitha to the former mourners alive, v. 41b. Elijah gave the resuscitated child to his mother (1 Kgs 17:23); Elisha presents the Shunammite woman's son to her (2 Kgs 4:36).[23]

Luke takes his audience into Jairus' room and allows them to see and hear the raising of the young girl. And while Peter placed everyone outside the upper room, Luke again lets his audience enter the upper room and see and hear Peter raising Tabitha.

23. Chance, *Acts*, 162.

Similarities between Elisha and Peter

Peter learned how to serve and minister by walking daily with Jesus and witnessing how Jesus served and ministered. Elijah also took Elisha under his wings and had Elisha walk daily with him and watch how he ministered as a prophet. When Elijah ascended to heaven Elisha continued the ministry of a prophet as he learned from Elijah as seen in the raising of the Shunammite's son in 2 Kings 4:8–37.

Both Elijah and Jesus are great examples of how important it is to mentor and to make disciples. They both understood that their ministry would one day end, but ministry for the people needed to continue, therefore they both chose individuals to mentor and follow in their footsteps. What the passages taught us is that Elisha and Peter learned from their mentors by being present and observant in order to serve and do ministry.

It is also worth noting that when Elisha raised the Shunammite's son, he had already received Elijah's double share of his spirit. Not only did Elisha learn then from Elijah about ministry, but also shared in Elijah's double share of the spirit. Also the way Peter raised Tabitha was not only similar to Jesus, but also to Elijah and Elisha. Just as Jesus' ministry from his birth on was by the Holy Spirit, so Peter's ministry after the ascension of Jesus was under the power of the Holy Spirit. Discipleship and mentoring does not only mean to just follow someone and learn from them, but to also receive the presence of the Holy Spirit, who works through the mentor and the mentee. Therefore chapter four, the theological foundation will focus more fully on the role of the Holy Spirit in mentoring.

The life of a Christian is a life of discipleship and mentoring. When a Christian accepts the invitation to follow Jesus, she/he chooses to become a disciple of Jesus Christ. Yet Christ also calls individuals into leadership roles, they are to be mentored for the call of leadership. A Christian is to learn discipleship from Scripture, from faithful disciples like Elijah, Elisha, Peter and from the great disciple-maker himself, Jesus Christ. Potential Christian leaders in the faith also need mature, seasoned, experienced mentors to teach them how to become effective leaders and disciple makers. Disciples makers, disciples, mentors and mentees also need to pray for the working of the Holy Spirit, who worked in the life of Jesus and of Peter.

In the life of the church then, it is important to have seasoned, experienced Christians to mentor younger Christians as they journey together through life. Mike Slaughter writes:

> All people are equally important to God, but all people are not equally strategic to the investment of our time for God's mission. Jesus ministered to the multitudes, but he strategically spent the majority of his time mentoring his twelve disciples. The ultimate test of success is not what we accomplish or achieve but whom we develop."[24]

Mentoring would be beneficial by pairing people that have similar passions of ministry, so that they could work together, the younger and less experienced learning from the more experienced Christian. The lessons would not take place in a classroom setting, but through fellowship, not through preaching, but through life experience. As Elisha journeyed with Elijah, and as Peter fellowshipped with Jesus, so seasoned and experienced church members are to mentor and disciple newly baptized church members, and young people, under the leading of the Holy Spirit, to carry on the gospel message. In the next chapter we will look at an example of mentorship within the early Seventh-day Adventist movement. We will see how James White effectively mentored John Nevins Andrews as the young Seventh-day Adventist denomination was forming.

24. Slaughter, *Momentum for Life*, 79, 80.

Chapter 4

Mentoring in Early Seventh-day Adventism

James White and John Nevins Andrews

Leadership development through the process of mentoring is one significant way of helping individuals grow into strong and successful leaders. Within the development of the Seventh-day Adventist denomination, there are numerous examples of experienced leaders mentoring young people for the ministry. The purpose of this chapter is to explore how James White, one of the pioneers of the Seventh-day Adventist church, mentored John Nevins Andrews, who became one of the most prominent scholars of early Seventh-day Adventism.

James White began mentoring young John Andrews when he and his wife moved in with Andrews' parents in November of 1850. He encouraged young John to start visiting the local communities and preach the gospel. James also loaned him his horse, Charlie, in order to be able to travel and preach. As James White began the periodical *Review and Herald* he invited John to write articles for the periodical. This began the writing career of young John that continued the rest of his life.

As James moved away from John's parents, the mentoring of young John continued. Whenever John needed to regroup, rest, and recuperate from his busy preaching schedule, he would often come to the home of James. James would encourage him, take care of him, give him the best room in the house and help Andrews regain his health to continue his ministry. When the new denomination faced doctrinal differences such as when to keep the Sabbath, or needed a representative for her beliefs, James would often recommend John for the task. Though their friendship was tried many times over differences, when John was asked to be the first missionary to Europe, he relied greatly on the wisdom and mentorship of James.

James White

Seventh-day Adventism was born out of the Great Disappointment of the Millerite movement. William Miller was an American Baptist preacher who believed from his study of the book of Daniel that Jesus would return from heaven to earth in the mid-1800s. One of the preachers within the Millerite movement, Samuel S. Snow, set the date of Jesus' return to October 22, 1844.[1] The followers of William Miller came to be known as Millerites, or Advent believers. When Jesus did not return on that date, the bitter experience came to be known as the Great Disappointment.[2] Some leaders and preachers from the Great Disappointment of the 1844 Millerite movement became the founders of the Seventh-day Adventist denomination. One of those preachers was James White, who would become a mentor of other young people in the newly formed denomination. One of the young people who James White mentored was John Nevins Andrews.

James Springer White was born August 4, 1821 in the township of Palmyra, Somerset County, Maine. James was the middle child of nine born to John and Betsey White. He passed away

1. Maxwell, *Tell it to the World*, 63.
2. Ibid.

August 6, 1881 at Battle Creek Sanitarium in Battle Creek, Michigan at age sixty.

James grew up in the state of Maine to a farmer who had been tilling his own soil fifteen years by the time James was born. John White, James' father, was a religious man, who taught voice, had morning and evening worships, and served as a deacon for 40 years in the Christian Connexion denomination. Three sons of John White would go on to become ministers, one a Baptist minister, another a minister for the Methodist Episcopal Church, and, James, a minister for the Christian Connexion denomination and then for the Seventh-day Adventist denomination.[3] James' education was short-lived because he was a sickly child. Around the age of three, he was diagnosed with form fever causing him to have seizures. Though he recovered, he suffered from crossed eyes. Because of his condition, he dropped out of school to work on the farm believing that he would be illiterate the rest of his life. As he grew, his eyesight improved, so at the age of nineteen he enrolled at the local academy of St. Albans, Maine. The school term only lasted twelve weeks. In order to continue his education, he enrolled for a three-month term at the Methodist Episcopal School in Reedfield, Maine. His whole formal education consisted of twelve weeks of elementary school and twenty-nine weeks beyond that.[4]

The parents of James accepted the teachings of William Miller. At first, James thought that Miller's ideas were fanatical. "But when James White's mother supported Millerism, her son had to take it seriously. She calmly answered his objections. Soon he began to come under a growing conviction that Miller might be right."[5] He was so convinced of the soon return of Jesus that he felt he should preach it. He announced a religious meeting in the Troy, Maine townhouse and gave preaching a try. After attempting to speak for a while, he became confused. In embarrassment, he gave up and sat down. Some time later he tried again, only to speak for twenty minutes, and, in confusion to sit down again. However, James did

3. Wheeler, *James White*, 22.

4. Ibid., 22–23.

5. Ibid., 23.

not give up but rather analyzed his failure and went on a preaching tour for the communities along the Kennebec River. "Reports indicate that during the winter months of 1842–1843 more than 1,000 people responded to his preaching. A few days after he returned to Palmyra the Christian Connexion ordained him to the ministry."[6] However, after the Great Disappointment of October 1844, James did not continue in the Christian Connexion denomination but became one of the three founders of Seventh-day Adventism. The other two founders were his wife, Ellen White, and Joseph Bates.[7] Without the leadership and organizational skills of James, there probably would not be a Seventh-day Adventist denomination. He founded the publishing work of the Seventh-day Adventist church, helped set up the organizational conference system that is still in use today, helped develop the health work, and also placed emphasis on the educational work of the church.

In March 1873, the General Conference session of the Seventh-day Adventist church voted to begin the Seventh-day Adventist Educational Society and James was voted president. This vote made him the nominal president of Battle Creek College that opened August 24, 1874 with 100 students. In 1880, James recommended that Sidney Brownsberger become the president of the college, who at the time served as the Principal of Battle Creek College. By 1881, Battle Creek College already had 490 students. Throughout his lifetime, he had not only been a minister, author, and theologian of the Seventh-day Adventist church, but also served as president of the denomination three times, for a total of ten years, spanning intermittently from May 17, 1865 to October 11, 1880.[8] James accomplished much for the organization of Seventh-day Adventism, but one of his greatest accomplishments was his love for young people and finding leaders to mentor who where committed to the work of the Lord. One author described him in the following way: "One of James' great strengths was his ability to gather about him young people whom he inspired with

6. Wheeler, *James White*, 27.

7. Knight, *Joseph Bates*, ix.

8. Wheeler, *James White*, 139.

his own enthusiasm for the cause of God and a willingness to make any sacrifice necessary to advance it."[9] One such young person that he had a great influence upon was John Nevins Andrews.

John Nevins Andrews

John was eight years younger than James. George Knight, a retired professor of church history of the Seventh-day Adventist denomination who taught at the Theological Seminary at Andrews University, stated, "John Nevins Andrews was the foremost scholar of the young Seventh-day Adventist Church."[10] In fact, Andrews University, a gem of Seventh-day Adventism, located at Berrien Springs, Michigan, is named after John Nevins Andrews. John was not only a great scholar, but also an important editor for the *Review and Herald* periodical from 1859 to 1862; the President of the Denomination from May 14, 1867 to May 12, 1868; and the first foreign missionary sent by the church to Europe from 1874 until his death.[11] However, John Andrews would not have accomplished any of these leadership roles without the mentoring and trust of James to empower him with leadership roles. On July 3, 1868, in a letter to James and Ellen White, John expressed his appreciation for James because of his willingness "to counsel me in any way, or to reprove me sharply, or to express [his] fears of my course."[12] This is an indication that he looked up to the counsel of James throughout his lifetime.

John Nevins Andrews was born July 22, 1829 in Poland, Maine, but he grew up in Paris, Maine with his parents and brother, William, who was two years younger. Growing up, he faithfully attended the Methodist church with his parents. From a young age, it seems John had a thirst for knowledge and for Scripture by paying attention to the preacher. In fact, he remembers a time at church

9. Robinson, *James White*, 84.

10. Knight, *Lest We Forget*, 135.

11. Steinweg, "In Defense of the Truth," 5.

12. Smoot, "The Churchman," 45.

one day when he was only five years old and the pastor preached on Revelation 20:11, "Then I saw a great white throne and the one who sat on it; the earth and the heaven fled from his presence, and no place was found for them." John made the comment at one time that he rarely read Revelation 20:11 and did not think of the sermon he heard at age five.[13] This is a significant memory for a religious event that happened at such a young age.

Neither John, his brother, nor his father had good health. Since William Andrews was crippled, and his father was not in good health, John took upon himself the responsibility of helping his father on the New England farm. He quit school at the age of eleven and all that he learned afterwards was what he studied on his own. His uncle Charles was hoping to help him get back to school and study law, but God had other plans for young John.[14] Consequently, John gave his life to be led by the Lord and not by worldly allurements. The early education that he received was enough to give him a thirst to continue studying and educating himself. Some would consider his lack of formal education a hindrance. Perhaps so, but "as an adult John could read the Bible in seven languages and claimed the ability to reproduce the New Testament from memory."[15] That, plus everything else he accomplished in his short life, showed his thirst for knowledge and the impact mentorship can have in a person's life.

At the age of fourteen, with his family, he accepted William Miller's teaching of Jesus' return. As he was walking with Davis, a fellow Millerite believer, to an advent meeting, they were crossing a bridge in Paris, Maine when a mob threatened the worshippers. A man from the mob began hitting Davis with a horsewhip, but John jumped in and put his arms around Davis and said, "We are commanded to bear one another's burdens. If you whip Brother Davis, you must whip me also."[16] This reaction confounded the man who

13. Steinweg, "In Defense of the Truth," 1.

14. Foster, "Andrews & His Family," 6.

15. Knight, *Lest We Forget*, 135.

16. Ibid.

did not want to whip a boy, so he stopped and let them through the bridge. This experience exemplifies the courage of young John.

Thoroughly discouraged that Jesus did not come in 1844 and young, he did not give up hope in God or in Scripture. His father Edward Andrews invited another discouraged family, the Stowells, to move in with them. Fifteen-year-old Marion, who was the daughter of the Stowells, read a tract on the subject of the Sabbath written by Thomas M. Preble, a Millerite preacher. She shared the tract with her older brother Oswald, who shared it with John. The teenagers made a decision together to honor the Lord by keeping the Sabbath. So they tried to finish their chores, like wood splitting and baking, on Friday so that they would keep the Sabbath on Saturday. Soon, seven families in Paris, Maine accepted the Sabbath truth and kept the Sabbath on Saturday.[17] There were great doctrinal disagreements between the Sabbath-keepers so that after a while some decided to stay away from the group just so they would not have to deal with the controversies. In 1849, Stockbridge Howland, James and Ellen White decided to visit Paris, Maine. They were to encourage the believers and see what they could do to bring about unity. It was at this visit that John considered the time of his conversion.[18] Present at that meeting was a man by the name of F. T. Howland (not related to Stockbridge Howland), who disrupted the meeting trying to cause problems. Stockbridge Howland fell on his knees and started praying. After he prayed, he got off his knees and said to the troublemaker, "You have torn the hearts of God's children and made them bleed. Leave this house, or God will smite you."[19] F. T. Howland was so stunned by this rebuke that he quickly fled the place and never bothered the believers again. That meeting had such a powerful impact on John that he exclaimed, "I would exchange a thousand errors for one truth."[20] When John made this statement he was twenty years old. He was very impressed and inspired by the leadership and pres-

17. Wheeler, *James White*, 58.

18. Ibid., 59.

19. Ibid., 58.

20. Steinweg, "In Defense of the Truth," 4.

ence of James at that meeting. Their friendship lasted a lifetime even though it was tested at times.

James Mentoring John

The mentoring process of John by James began in November of 1850 when James and Ellen White moved to Paris, Maine and took up residence in the home of Edward Andrews. James did not move into the home of Edward Andrews to mentor his son John, but took the opportunity to do so. Further support for the mentorship that took place between James and John was recorded in what was written about their friendship:

> John Andrews soon became attracted to James White. With the encouragement of the older man, he began preaching in surrounding towns and villages. The accession of this aggressive scholarly young man represented, as James White wrote, 'no small reinforcement.'[21]

The confidence that James had in John was strengthened in January of 1851 when he lent him his horse, Charlie, with his carriage to go with Samuel Rhodes and visit Advent believers in northern Vermont and Canada.[22] When James began to publish the periodical *Review and Herald* in Rochester, the first printing on May 6, 1852, he had on its masthead as part of the publishing committee Joseph Bates, John Nevins Andrews, and Joseph Baker.[23] This was the kind of faith that he had in young John. As a part of mentoring John, James' placed him in leadership roles. As John proved faithful in these leadership roles, James, in 1853, ordained young twenty-four year old John Andrews.[24] This was a significant moment in their relationship and John's spiritual maturity.

While James and Ellen White lived with Edward Andrews, something happened that caused a rift between Edward Andrews

21. Robinson, *James White*, 68.
22. White, *Ellen G. White*, 205.
23. Wheeler, *James White*, 71.
24. Steinweg, "In Defense of the Truth," 4.

and James. This rift continued the rest of Edward Andrews' life and at times it affected the relationship between John and James. Not only did Edward Andrews have hard feelings toward James, he also started spreading the rumor that James cheated him out of eight dollars while living at his house.[25] In his own defense, James claimed that the only reason Edward Andrews made that accusation was because he did not want to accept the leadership of Ellen White as a prophet. James remarked that he had helped Edward Andrews' son so much, including financially, and could that gratitude not cause respect and acknowledgment of good will?[26] Clearly, at times, the relationship between James and John was cold. However, they still loved each other dearly. "John would sometimes address his letters to him and Ellen 'Very dear Brother and Sister White' and sign them with 'much love.'"[27] This shared love was evident for John as well.

In the summer of 1854, John burned out from so much preaching and traveling that he went and found refuge and rest with James as he recovered. After his recovery, John threw himself into incessant labor in the ministry only to be burned out again and return to James' home at Rochester, New York. "Early in 1855, J. N. Andrews arrived at the Rochester house. He was completely broken in health, scarcely able to speak above a whisper, and with seriously damaged eyesight. He suffered from insomnia, depression, and stomach trouble."[28] John was only twenty-six years old at the time and to recover White gave him the best room in the house, fed him, and took care of him. He even appealed on his behalf in the *Review and Herald* in order to raise money to buy John good quality clothes. James not only appealed on his behalf, he led the pledge to raise money for John with his own pledge of one hundred dollars.[29]

25. Graybill, "The Family Man," 18–19.

26. Wheeler, *James White*, 106.

27. Ibid., 73.

28. Robinson, *James White*, 108.

29. Graybill, "The Family Man," 19.

John was so sick, though, that he decided to return home to his father at Paris, Maine. Before the year 1855 ended, the Andrews family with several other families moved from Paris, Maine to Waukon, Iowa. As the family was passing through Battle Creek, Michigan on their way to Iowa, John placed in the hands of James an article on when the Sabbath should be observed. They observed the Sabbath on Saturday, but the young Advent believers did not know what time to begin the Sabbath. Some kept the Sabbath from 6 p.m. Friday to 6 p.m. Saturday on the insistence of Joseph Bates. Others kept it from sunrise Saturday to sunrise Sunday, and yet others from sunset Friday to sunset Saturday. James thought that this disharmony in Sabbath keeping was not good for the Advent believers, so he asked John to study the subject from the Bible and come to a conclusion.[30] James had great respect for John and now he was not asking him in order to get young John involved in the ministry, but to help share the burden of the ministry as a trusted and respected scholar and leader.

John did study the Sabbath and the article he left with James on the way to Iowa was the results of his study. From his study, he came to the conclusion that the Sabbath should be observed from sunset Friday to sunset Saturday. Since then, Seventh-day Adventists have observed the Sabbath from sunset Friday to sunset Saturday.[31] This reveals the faith that James and all the other leaders within the denomination had in John as a theologian. This was not the only time that James and the leaders of Seventh-day Adventists would call on John to study a subject from the Bible for clarity. The next issue that James asked John to study was the subject of tithing, for the young denomination had no system set up for paying the few ministers in the ministry field.

Prior to John's assignment in January of 1859 to study this topic, James and Ellen White had to make a dangerous trip to Waukon, Iowa in the winter of 1856 in order to call John Andrews and John Loughborough back into the ministry. Since both of them had burned out from so much preaching, writing, and traveling,

30. Knight, *Joseph Bates*, 158–62.

31. White, *Ellen G. White*, vol. 1, 322–23.

they went to rest, but when health was restored they remained home. Regarding their reputation, Gerald Wheeler states that the "Andrews and Stevens families had poisoned the minds of many families at Waukon and elsewhere."[32] Negative views of James and Ellen White by the Advent believers in Waukon were most likely because of the rift that existed between Edward Andrews and James White.

Ellen White reports the following of their arrival to Waukon: "We reached Waukon Wednesday night, and found nearly all the Sabbathkeepers sorry that we had come. Much prejudice existed against us, for much had been said concerning us calculated to injure our influence."[33] Wheeler seems to explain the reason for their cold reception in his biography of James White: "In time he learned that one of the strongest grudges the Waukon believers held against him was that he had moved the Review from Rochester to Battle Creek. But that was not the only problem. The bitterness and hostility that had erupted in Paris, Maine, was still lurking beneath the surface."[34]

After spending some time with the "Sabbathkeepers," as she referred to the Advent believers, and explaining why they moved the Review from Rochester to Battle Creek, peace was made and both Loughborough and John Andrews returned to the ministry. Loughborough returned to work at Battle Creek and John started conducting meetings around the Waukon area. Though there was reconciliation again between the Andrews and White families, resentment in the heart of John towards James still lingered. "Andrews was again in full-time evangelism, but the feelings his father and in-laws held against the Whites were still at work. Both he and Uriah and Harriet Smith—his brother and sister-in-law—still rankled over the incidents in Maine."[35] It seems that it was very hard for the Andrews family, including John, to let go of the way

32. Wheeler, *James White*, 104.

33. White, *Ellen G. White*, vol. 1, 348.

34. Wheeler, *James White*, 102.

35. Ibid., 103.

James White left things in Paris, Maine when they moved out of Edward Andrews' home.

It was at this time that Ellen White told her husband to call John Andrews from Waukon, Iowa to come to Battle Creek, Michigan and hold a Bible study on tithing in order to set up financial support for the ministers.[36] John came to Battle Creek and held a two-day Bible study on tithing in mid-January 1859. The result of those studies led to a tithing system that they called Systematic Benevolence. This tithing system "encouraged men to contribute 5 to 25 cents per week, and women 2 to 10 cents. Beyond that, the plan assessed both men and women 1 to 5 cents per week for each $100 of property they might own."[37] So far, in addition to the issue of tithing, John did an in-depth study on the question of when the Sabbath should begin. This led James in 1859 to refer to him as "our theologian."[38] Yet there were other questions that "our theologian" needed to study. When the American Civil War broke out in 1861, the young church was faced with its young men being drafted into the war. The issues of killing and noncombatant status were brought up. Whenever a Seventh-day Adventist was drafted, they could pay three hundred dollars to excuse the person from being drafted into the war. By mid-1864, the war had accelerated and the payment of three hundred dollars to be excused was only for those with noncombatant status. John was asked to lead the way in obtaining the needed noncombatant status from Washington D.C. He was hoping that James would accompany him to Washington D.C. for the meeting, but because of James' schedule he could not go with him. However, he did stop by Rochester to meet and pray with John in preparation for his trip to Washington D.C. He also went downtown with John and spent fifty dollars to purchase a new suit for him to wear at his upcoming meeting.[39] John went in August of 1864 to Washington D.C. and was successful in obtaining the noncombatant status for the young Seventh-day Adventist

36. White, *Ellen G. White*, vol. 1, 387–388.

37. Wheeler, *James White*, 123.

38. Smoot, "Andrews' Role in Seventh-day Adventist History," 8.

39. Graybill, "The Family Man," 31.

denomination. In May 1866, it was voted at the General Conference Committee in business session that John would prepare an article "setting for the teachings of the Scriptures on the subject of war."[40]

In 1867, another Sabbath question came up for the Seventh-day Adventist believers. "In March 1867, the United States purchased the Alaska Territory from Russia. Because the Russians had come to Alaska from the west and the Americans from the east, Russian time in Alaska was twenty-four hours ahead of American time there."[41] That confused some Seventh-day Adventist believers when it came to the observance of the Sabbath, because the Americans would be keeping their Sabbath on Saturday while the same day for the Russians would actually be Sunday. They turned to John's study of the subject and bring clarity to this confusion. He wrote an article entitled "The Definite Seventh Day: Or, God's Measurement of Time on the Round World."[42] Once again, his leadership and scholarship helped to resolve what was a serious theological conflict for Seventh-day Adventist believers.

In 1872, again, the General Conference Committee turned to John to study Christian Education from the Bible and bring recommendations on how to start up a Seventh-day Adventist College.[43] This revealed that James' respect for John as a theologian kept growing. September 1870, James through the *Review* invited two hundred individuals to donate about ten dollars each so that John could purchase books for his personal library in order to finish his book on the topic of the Sabbath.[44]

40. White, *Ellen G. White: The Progressive Years*, vol. 2, 136.

41. Cottrell, "The Theologian of the Sabbath," 108.

42. The article was published in the *Review and Herald*, February 14, 1871, p. 65.

43. Robinson, *John Nevins Andrews: Flame for the Lord*, 77.

44. Smoot, "The Churchman," 48.

The First Official Missionary Overseas

The Seventh-day Adventist denomination was growing in the United States and set its sight on Europe in the middle of the 1870s. Many in leadership wanted to send John to Europe, but James was hesitant. As it was stated earlier, because of the rift between James and Edward Andrews, at times, it affected the relationship between James and John. Even though Edward Andrews passed away in 1865, at times there were still disagreements and hard feelings between James and John. But from 1865 there were other reasons for hard feelings between the two.

"In August 1865, [James] suffered a severe stroke of paralysis from which the physicians gave little hope of recovery. James did survive, but from that point onward the overworked and overburdened denominational leader suffered the effects of broken health. At times, they made him moody and difficult to live and work with."[45] Between the first stroke of 1865 to his death in 1881, James experienced at least five strokes, but that first stroke was the most severe. "That stroke and his inability to trust others, slow down, or delegate authority colored the remainder of his life. Problems that had been evident in his early years became pronounced after 1865. Thus, he suffered from recurring depression, was suspicious of other people, and at times made ill-advised statements and accusations."[46] One church leader that received a sharp censure from James after his first stroke was Uriah Smith, a brother-in-law of John. Uriah Smith took over the publishing association during the years of 1866 to 1869 while James was recovering from his stroke. Under the leadership of Uriah Smith, the publishing association ended up in a financial mess, James censured Uriah Smith so harshly that it caused a major rift between them.[47] There was a rift not only between Uriah Smith and James but also between James and John.

45. Knight, *Meeting Ellen White*, 59–60.

46. Knight, *Walking With Ellen White*, 73–74.

47. Smoot, "The Churchman," 49.

> White's severe criticism of Smith precipitated a rift that widened over the next four years to an unbridgeable chasm. Uriah declared in 1869 that if the two could not cooperate, he recognized that it was his responsibility to leave Battle Creek, rather than James White. The year's absence from the editorial office in 1869–1870 only delayed the impending clash. The breach became irreparable in 1873 when Uriah questioned the authority of James White to hold a privileged position as counselor to the others. Butler had tried in the early months of 1873 to get the Whites reconciled not only to Smith but to Andrews as well. Early in 1873, Andrews wrote James White that he had prayed for him each day since they had parted Battle Creek.[48]

The rift between John and the Whites was over a letter that Ellen White wrote to John. "[Ellen White] sent a testimony of reproof because of her feeling that Andrews devoted too much time to intellectual investigation and study. She felt he should concentrate on becoming a better balanced person."[49] Because of this rift between the Whites and John, they did not heartily recommend John as a missionary to Europe, not until George Butler sat down with Uriah Smith, John, and the Whites and reconciliation was made. This reconciliation helped to rekindle James and John's relationship.

After the reconciliation, James and Ellen White gave their blessing to John to go to Europe and in 1874 John sailed to Europe as the first official missionary of the Seventh-day Adventist denomination. While in Europe, John Andrews "asked for James White's advice on all aspects of the European work."[50] James had a great deal of experience in starting up the Seventh-day Adventist denomination in North America, with the publishing work as well as with his organizational skills. It is no surprise that John would seek advice from James in starting up the Seventh-day Adventist Church in Europe.

48. Ibid., 49–50.

49. Ibid., 48.

50. Smoot, "The Churchman," 57.

James responded enthusiastically to John and supported him greatly with his own finances, with advice, and by asking the Seventh-day Adventist members in North America to donate funds to the European mission. "In May, 1876, he launched a campaign to raise $10,000 to equip a printing plant in Switzerland 'under the care of our worthy missionary, Elder J. N. Andrews.'"[51] Ellen White wrote to the new believers in Switzerland: "We sent you the ablest man in all our ranks."[52]

Throughout the years that they knew each other, James and John loved and respected each other greatly. At times, their relationship was tested by early misunderstandings in Maine, James' stroke that led him to become harsh, and letters of counsel from the Whites that were sometimes not received well from John. Yet, John would still look up to White for wisdom and leadership especially when he was pioneering the growth of the Seventh-day Adventist denomination in Europe. When James became very sick in 1865 after his first major stroke, he asked for John to come and pray for him, this was the confidence and respect that he had for John.[53] James also had great respect for John as a theologian, author, writer, preacher, and spiritual man.

Three years after John prayed for James' healing, James would say the following about John:

> Brother Andrews is a man of God. He is a close Bible student. He walks with God, and shares largely of the Holy Spirit direct from the throne. Brother and Sister White, especially when groaning under responsibilities and trials, often find relief in counseling with Brother Andrews and listening to words of wisdom from his lips.[54]

The last time that James and John would see each other was when John came back to America because his daughter was very sick. He brought her back to Battle Creek Sanitarium, they arrived

51. Ibid., 58.
52. Steveny, "Andrews' Personal Library," 152.
53. Wheeler, *James White*, 165.
54. Robinson, *James White*, 315.

October 4, 1878 and his daughter, Mary Andrews died November 27 at the age of 17 from tuberculosis. John stayed in America until April of 1879 and preached his last sermon in America at the Dime Tabernacle Seventh-day Adventist Church in Battle Creek to a crowd of three thousand.[55] Ellen White pleaded with him not to return to Europe until he was fully recovered, for he also was sick. His heart was in Europe and spreading the gospel there, so he headed back to Europe and also died from tuberculosis October 21, 1883 at the age of fifty-five. However, John outlived the great leader whom he respected and looked up to since James passed away August 6, 1881 at the age of sixty.

> John Andrews lived to write James White's obituary. To Andrews, his friend was "in an eminent sense a minister of Christ. He did not shrink from toil, from sacrifice, nor from reproach." Referring to more than 30 years of intimate association with him, "we bear testimony to his excellence as a man, a Christian, and a minister of the Word of God." Andrews singled out White's talent for business management, declaring that "the work accomplished in America under his general supervision" was "a monument which can never be overthrown." Beyond that, Andrews noted his "deep interest in the mission of the Seventh-day Adventists in Europe.[56]

It is evident that James was a great influence and mentor to John. It was with the encouragement of James that John began to travel in sharing the gospel. It was James who also loaned his horse to John in order to be able to travel around the towns learning how to preach the gospel. James also gave opportunities to John to write articles for the newly founded periodical, beginning John's literary ministry. When John needed rest and recuperation, it was often found in the home of his mentor. When James needed someone to study denominational doctrines, he relied on the wisdom of John. When John went to Europe as the first missionary of the Seventh-day Adventist denomination, it was the counsel of James that

55. Robinson, *John Nevins Andrews: Flame for the Lord*, 111.

56. Smoot, "The Churchman," 63.

he often sought in pioneering the work of the gospel in Europe. Clearly, through all these examples, the mentorship of James was very influential on the life of John.

Current and Potential Mentoring in Seventh-day Adventism

Since the time of James mentoring John, mentoring has been used within the Seventh-day Adventist denomination in different parts of the world to adequately train young people. The Seventh-day Adventist Church in Germany organized the Institute for Continuing Education in order to mentor pastoral interns. This mentoring process rests upon four pillars: training mentors, educating interns, cooperating with local conferences, and selecting local churches. In conclusion, "this mentoring concept, after 12 years of implementation, has proved to be successful. The process has become more satisfying for both mentors and mentees. Leadership skills of the mentors have advanced, and mentees feel better supervised."[57] Therefore, mentoring has proven successful with pastoral interns in Germany as it has in the life of John Andrews.

In the Ohio Conference of Seventh-day Adventists, mentoring has become important to the youth department. In 2014, a pilot program began for mentoring young people. The mentoring includes church members choosing a young person to mentor. They would in turn daily pray for the young person, weekly touch base with the young person, at church welcome them and greet them, monthly invite the young person with a couple of their friends out to lunch, and yearly buy a present for the young person on their birthday.[58] In chapter eight, more will be discussed on the continuation of youth mentoring in the Ohio Conference of Seventh-day Adventists.

Therefore, there are many lessons that we could learn regarding mentoring. To apply the lessons of mentoring from James White, leaders can be trained to develop others through the

57. Fischer, "Mentoring Interns and Young Pastors," 16.

58. Information about the Youth Mentoring Program may be found at the Web site http://ohiosdayouth.org.

process of mentoring in small groups. First of all, the leaders of small groups would personally seek out and invite individuals into the group to mentor. If James did not have a passion to mentor and encourage young people to enter the ministry, John Nevins Andrews would probably not have been a great theologian of the Seventh-day Adventist denomination. There is need for mature, spiritual leaders to not only be busy doing the work of the Lord, or discipling believers in following Christ, but also be involved in recognizing spiritual gifts in young people, encouraging and empowering them through mentoring in the ministry.

Second, leaders of the small groups are to help mentees develop their leadership skills by using their spiritual gifts through serving in the community and learning to lead small groups, either through a soup kitchen, singing in nursing homes, Habitat for Humanity projects, gardening, or another avenue. Each small group would serve together, mentors along with mentees. Mentorship does not necessarily have to take place only between people of the same spiritual gifts. While James White had the gifts of administration and starting up institutions, John Andrews had the gift of studying biblical doctrine meticulously and drawing sound, balanced conclusions that benefited early Seventh-day Adventism greatly. Yet James White was able to mentor, advise, and involve John Andrews in using the spiritual gifts that the Holy Spirit had gifted him. So, it is with modern mentorship, leaders do not necessarily need to mentor individuals who have the same spiritual gifts, but they are to look to mentor individuals who have the same passions and passion for Jesus Christ.

Third, leaders of the small groups are to genuinely care for the needs of the mentees. It is hard for a church to find ways to help, encourage, and support members who are struggling or discouraged. Small groups are one way to have leaders recognize needs and give support and encouragement. Just as John Andrews felt comfortable turning to James White for help when he was sick and burnt out, so mentees would turn to their mentors for support and encouragement. The mentor would bring needs to the rest of the church body for greater support when needed.

Lastly, it is natural for the mentor and the mentee to have moments when they may be at odds. As is the case with John and James, they experience moments of disagreement and times of silence. But they worked through these things and when it is all said and done, they put the kingdom of God above themselves and worked together in order to spread the gospel message. Mentorship does not mean that the mentor and the mentee will not have disagreements, or even significant arguments. In fact, it is healthy for individuals to share concerns and problems with each other honestly in order to learn and develop.

In conclusion, leadership development through mentoring is an effective way of encouraging and preparing others to successfully serve the Lord and lead others in serving the Lord. Leaders are to initiate the process of mentoring by inviting individuals to join them in service. They are to support and encourage mentees in their walk with the Lord and in their service for the Lord. Part of the support is honesty, openness, and the willingness to work through misunderstandings instead of giving up on people or relationships. When leaders are developed through mentoring, more individuals share the burden of service and the mission of the church is accomplished more effectively.

Another important aspect of mentoring is the role of the Holy Spirit in the life of the mentor and the mentee. This I call mentoring by the design of the Holy Spirit. Chapter five will deal with the Holy Spirit as the theological foundation of mentoring and discipleship. When leaders are developed through Spirit led mentoring, more individuals share the burden of service and the mission of the church is accomplished more effectively.

Chapter 5

Mentoring by the Design of the Holy Spirit

The Role of the Holy Spirit in Mentoring

THE WORK OF THE Holy Spirit is essential in effective mentoring and discipleship. In this chapter we explore the role of the Holy Spirit in mentoring and discipling. We examine the history of the Christian church in trying to understand and explain the work of the Holy Spirit. Then, we'll look at three reasons why the Holy Spirit is very important in the life of the Christian. The three reasons why the Holy Spirit is important have to do with Christology (the study of the doctrine of Jesus Christ), soteriology (the study of the doctrine of salvation), and ecclesiology (the study of the church). Discipling and mentoring have to do with leading people to experience salvation, follow Christ, and to serve with other believers from a church, yet it is the leading of the Holy Spirit that makes effective the work of salvation, following Christ, and serving through a local church community. Therefore, as the theological implications of the role of the Holy Spirit are explored, it will be important to note that pneumatology (the study of the doctrine of the Holy Spirit) is just as important as Christology, inextricably connected to soteriology, and the basis for genuine community among Christians.

Furthermore, the role of the Holy Spirit in effective discipleship ministry to youth will be explored as well as how the Holy Spirit uses discipleship for transformation not only of the disciple, but also of communities and neighborhoods where the disciple of Christ lives. At the end, this work will show the great impact of mentorship and discipleship on individual disciples and the Church as a whole.

History of Pneumatology

Historically, the Christian Church struggled to ascertain the identity of the Holy Spirit. For the early church, the event of Pentecost was still fresh. However, the identity of the Holy Spirit was not clarified. When the Council of Nicea met in 325 AD, it affirmed the Holy Spirit in the statement, "and we believe in the Holy Spirit." No other explanation was given about the Holy Spirit, whether the Spirit was fully God or not. In 381 AD, the Council of Constantinople determined that the Spirit "proceeds from the Father through [or "and" in the Western church][1] the Son."[2]

Tyron Inbody sheds light on this struggle to understand the Holy Spirit. He states that "the theologians at Constantinople struggled to rank the Holy Spirit equal with the Father and the Son. Although none of them applied the word *homoousia* (same substance) to the Spirit, they applied narrative language to affirm that the Spirit is fully and equally the Spirit of God."[3] Stanley J. Grenz states that from the Second Ecumenical Council in Constantinople in 381, "the orthodox understanding of God would need to view all three persons—Father, Son, and Spirit—as fully divine."[4] The way Christians understand the relationship between

1. For greater in depth explanation of the controversial positions between the Eastern and Western church, see Seitzer, *Nicene Christianity*, 154.

2. Inbody, *The Faith of the Christian Church*, 248–49.

3. Ibid., 249.

4. Grenz, *Theology for the Community of God*, 60.

the Father, Son and Holy Spirit, i.e. the Holy Trinity, is highly sensitive and has a direct impact on the potential for Christianity to be viewed as a polytheistic religion. Therefore, it is important for this language to point to the unity and ultimate singleness of the Godhead.

Three theologians who give a clearer understanding of the relationship among the Father, Son, and Holy Spirit are Basil, Gregory of Nyssa, and Gregory of Nazianzus. "Their efforts [have given] birth to what [has] became the classic formulation of the doctrine of the Trinity."[5] Yet, even with a clearer understanding of the Trinity, much about the Holy Spirit remains a mystery. One of the pioneers of the Seventh-day Adventist church sums it up this mystery in the following words:

> The nature of the Holy Spirit is a mystery. Men [sic] cannot explain it, because the Lord has not revealed it to them. Men [sic] having fanciful views may bring together passages of Scripture and put a human construction on them, but the acceptance of these views will not strengthen the church. Regarding such mysteries, which are too deep for human understanding, silence is golden.[6]

Much mystery still revolves around the Holy Spirit and there are some things as Ellen White has come to conclude that we will never understand about the Holy Spirit. Although there are disagreements about the Holy Spirit, like whether the Spirit proceeds from the Father and the Son or just the Father, all Christians should agree that the Holy Spirit is essential for the life of the Christian. Because "God continues to be present with us as the Spirit of Christ, creating a new community, empowering the people of God, nurturing the church in faithfulness, and leading us into lives of joy, peace, and love,"[7] the role of the Holy Spirit is crucial.

5. Ibid., 60.
6. White, *Acts of the Apostles*, 52.
7. Inbody, *The Faith of the Christian Church*, 249.

Three Reasons for Pneumatology in Discipling

When it comes to being a Christian, mentoring, and making disciples for Christ, the work of the Holy Spirit cannot be taken for granted. John Stott states, "The Christian life is life in the Spirit. All Christians are happily agreed about this. It would be impossible to be a Christian, let alone to live and grow as a Christian, without the ministry of the gracious Spirit of God. All we have and are as Christians we owe to him."[8] In addition, Tyron Inbody gives three reasons why the presence and theology of the Holy Spirit is so important for the Christian. The first reason, which is worth highlighting, is that "there is no Christology apart from pneumatology (doctrine of the Spirit)."[9] This is so true. A Christian, who is a devoted follower of Christ, is unable to be a Christian without the Holy Spirit's guidance, work, and influence. Christ's presence in the life of an individual and the Holy Spirit's guidance go together and are not to be separated. Stott says, "For to attempt to separate the Spirit of God from the Word of God (whether incarnate or written) has always been a foolish and dangerous mistake."[10] Inbody also makes this bold statement regarding Christology and pneumatology. "Without the power of the Spirit to make Christ present to the believer, he remains as a figure in the past without any significance other than as a historical example. Jesus Christ, who was raised by God, is alive in the church insofar as the Spirit instills and maintains his life in the community of his disciples."[11] In other words, Christ would only be a historical figure without the presence of the Holy Spirit in the lives of Christians.

Jürgen Moltmann writes about the connection between the Holy Spirit and Christ:

> We can see at a glance that the history of Christ and the history of the Holy Spirit are dovetailed and indissolubly intertwined: according to the Synoptic Gospels Christ

8. Stott, *Baptism and Fullness*, 3rd ed., 25.
9. Inbody, *The Faith of the Christian Church*, 247.
10. Stott, *Life in Christ*, 59.
11. Inbody, *The Faith of the Christian Church*, 247.

> comes from the Holy Spirit—"conceived by the Holy Spirit," baptized by the Holy Spirit—perform miracles and proclaims the kingdom of God in the power of the Spirit, surrenders himself to his redeeming death on the cross through the eternal Spirit, is raised by God through the life-giving Spirit, and in the Spirit is present among us now. *Christ's history in the Spirit* begins with his baptism and ends in his resurrection. Then things are reversed. Christ sends the Spirit upon the community of his people and is present in the Spirit. That is *the history of the Spirit in Christ.* The Spirit of God becomes the Spirit of Christ. The Christ sent in the Spirit becomes Christ the sender of the Spirit.[12]

Without the presence of the Holy Spirit believers would not experience the presence of the living Christ. This is because one role of the Holy Spirit is to guide people into truth, which is accomplished by glorifying Jesus for he is the truth.[13] But the Holy Spirit does not only guide us into a greater understanding of Christ and his message, but brings us to Christ himself, into a real and personal relationship with Jesus.[14] The Spirit was present with Christ throughout his ministry. Then, when Jesus ascended to heaven, he sent the Spirit to be present with all believers, and, through the Spirit, Jesus is present with all believers. Therefore, an important part of discipling and mentoring is helping individuals understand the work and role of the Holy Spirit in revealing Christ and helping to follow Christ.

The second reason why pneumatology is so important according to Inbody is because "the concepts of the Holy Spirit and salvation are inseparable."[15] Every aspect of our salvation is "launched and sealed by the Holy Spirit, who unites us with Christ in faith."[16] Without the Holy Spirit we would not experience conviction of sin, or receive the gift of repentance. We could not

12. Moltmann, *The Source of Life*, 17.

13. See John 16:12–15, 14:6.

14. Ministerial Association, *Seventh-day Adventists Believe*, 74.

15. Inbody, *The Faith of the Christian Church*, 247.

16. Ibid.

walk the path of sanctification if not for the guiding presence of the Holy Spirit. Along the same line of reasoning, Stanley J. Grenz states, "As the facilitator of new life, the Creator Spirit completes the saving activity of the triune God . . . Viewed from the perspective of God's ultimate intention for us, salvation is one divine act, the work of the Spirit in bringing us into full conformity with the likeness of Christ."[17] Clearly, salvation is experienced through the Holy Spirit. However, spiritual mentors have a role to play in the process as well. The Holy Spirit uses Christian teachers in order to lead individuals to Christ.[18]

The apostle Paul speaks of the need of individuals to minister salvation to those who do not know Christ. "But how are they to call on one in whom they have not believed? And how are they to believe in one whom they have never heard? And how are they to hear without someone to proclaim him?"[19] Individuals are used by the Holy Spirit to speak the good news and help people come to believe in Christ and experience salvation. Spiritual mentors, who have formed friendships with others, have an effective way of sharing the good news of salvation in Jesus Christ through the very relationship that is developed with the mentee. This is a model that comes directly from Jesus. Throughout his ministry, Jesus establishes a strong relationship with the disciples and countless others. It is largely the relational aspect of Jesus' ministry that moves people to experience salvation and intimacy with God.

"In conversion, the Spirit initiates us into the present experience of community."[20] From conversion, the Holy Spirit leads individuals into a community of believers. This is the third reason Inbody list as to why the Holy Spirit is important. "The church is created and maintained by the Holy Spirit from the time of the resurrection and Pentecost until all is complete."[21] Without the power of the Holy Spirit, the church becomes merely a human institution.

17. Grenz, *Theology for the Community of God*, 432–33.

18. Zuck, *Spirit-Filled Teaching*, 52.

19. Romans 10:14, NRSV.

20. Grenz, *Theology for the Community of God*, 438.

21. Inbody, *The Faith of the Christian Church*, 247.

LeRoy Froom asserts, "to depend on organization, or leaders, or wisdom of men [sic], is to put the human in place of the divine."[22] It is the Holy Spirit that gives life to the church, empowering the disciples to fulfill its mission that includes being faithful disciples and making disciples of Jesus Christ.

True communion in the church is experienced through the presence of the Holy Spirit. "The Spirit is the Spirit of communion. Spirit baptism implies communion."[23] Jan Paulsen, who is the retired president of the General Conference of Seventh-day Adventists, in an article that he wrote on the Holy Spirit states, "the Spirit will always lead us toward Christ and other people."[24] This statement underscores the fact that Christology and pneumatology go hand in hand, while simultaneously adding ecclesiology to the equation. "The community of God's people has always been the community of the Spirit."[25] Therefore, genuine community in the church is only possible by the Holy Spirit. For "the church is not just an association of individual believers but a participation in the Spirit in the loving communion enjoyed within God's triune life."[26] Humans are frail and "the presence of the Spirit is to make otherwise frail human beings into a genuine community of disciples."[27] Richard Rice in his book *The Reign of God* makes the point that especially in western Christianity the individual religious experience is so much stressed that sight for the community of the church is lost. He writes, "The primary manifestation of the power of the Spirit in this world is the presence of genuine Christian community."[28] This sense of authentic community is important because it reinforces the relational aspect of Christianity, which is made even more manifest through the incarnation of Jesus and the dynamics of the godhead.

22. Froom, *The Coming of the Comforter*, 66–67.

23. Macchia, *Baptized in the Spirit*, 156.

24. Paulsen, "The Holy Spirit—So What?" 8.

25. Ibid.

26. Macchia, *Baptized in the Spirit*, 164.

27. Ibid.

28. Rice, *The Reign of God*, 294.

The Holy Spirit is central to the community of the church, yet many in the Church are so focused on the individual Christian experience that genuine community is not grasped. In his book *The Body of Christ* on ecclesiology (the study of the doctrine of the Church), Reinder Bruinsma dedicates a chapter to the Holy Spirit, entitled "The Spirit in the Church."[29] He recognizes four "various aspects of the work of the Holy Spirit on behalf of the church and its members."[30] These four aspects are as follows: "The Spirit gives us assurance of our adoption into God's family . . . The Spirit is the Spirit of truth . . . The Holy Spirit directs the proclamation of the gospel . . . Finally, the Spirit directs the worship of the church."[31] These four aspects of the Holy Spirit's work are important but what makes these aspects effective is mentoring. Although the Holy Spirit assures the believer of adoption, leads to truth, directs to proclaim the gospel, and is involved in the worship of the church, what helps an individual in recognizing the work of the Holy Spirit is a spiritual mentor. While Bruinsma does not mention discipleship and spiritual mentoring in his chapter on the Holy Spirit, it is implied that what is accomplished by the Holy Spirit is accomplished through disciples. "The apostles were able to face the spiritual elite because they were 'filled with the Holy Spirit.'[32] The members of the community of Christ believers in Jerusalem 'were all filled with the Holy Spirit and spoke the word of God boldly.'"[33] Bruinsma also notes the fact that Christ was filled with the Holy Spirit in the beginning of His ministry.[34] He continues to write; "the Gospel story provides abundant testimony that the Spirit indeed stayed with Jesus and that a new era had begun."[35] This indicates then that Jesus, filled by the Holy Spirit, choses disciples to follow Him. The community that Jesus created under the

29. Bruinsma, *The Body of Christ*.

30. Ibid., 74–75.

31. Ibid.

32. Acts 4:8 and 4:31 following.

33. Bruinsma, *The Body of Christ*, 77.

34. John 1:32.

35. Bruinsma, *The Body of Christ*, 76.

leading of the Holy Spirit was a community of disciples. Discipleship, then, is central to the work of the Holy Spirit as the Spirit creates a genuine community of believers.

Jason Vickers explains the role of the Holy Spirit as "divine physician."[36] He does this because "we routinely speak of the Spirit comforting us, healing our divisions, binding up our wounds, convicting us of our sins, assuring us of our forgiveness in Christ, and sanctifying us in the truth."[37] Vickers goes on to recognize the role of clergy and mature laity as midwives of the "divine physician," the Holy Spirit. "Also like an earthly physician, the Spirit routinely utilizes assistants in the work of healing. Thus, one can learn once again to think of clergy and mature believers in the church as attendees or midwives of the Holy Spirit."[38] In the context of this study, mentors can be viewed as midwives not so much from the perspective of the Holy Spirit healing people of diseases, although this happens in mentorship too, but more so from the perspective of aiding in the experience of rebirth and spiritual growth. While Vickers does not call this assistance to the Holy Spirit discipleship, these "midwives of the Holy Spirit" are discipling individuals within the community of believers.

The Holy Spirit and Youth Discipling

New believers and the youth of the church are in desperate need of spiritual midwives who are open to the leading of the Holy Spirit. The need for youth being discipled and mentored comes up often in many churches. In order to understand the problems and discern solutions for mentoring young people, it is helpful to turn to David Kinnaman, president of the Barna Group, who has conducted numerous studies to understand young people and has offered insightful solutions based on his research. He notes two facts about young people in the church. "1. Teenagers are some of

36. Vickers, *Minding the Good Ground*, 92.

37. Ibid., 92.

38. Ibid.

the most religiously active Americans. 2. American twenty somethings are the least religiously active."[39] His work shows "there is a 43 percent drop-off between the teen and early adult years in terms of church engagement."[40] This means that there is much work for the church when it comes to reaching this gap of non-religious Americans.

Kinnaman sees this problem in the church as the result of a lack of spiritual mentors who are guided by the Holy Spirit. "We need to allow the Holy Spirit to guide our parenting, our mentoring, and our friendships."[41] This means that discipleship and mentoring under the guidance of the Holy Spirit are possible solutions to aid in reengaging younger Christians and inspiring them to become active in the church. Spiritual mentors are Christian leaders who are open to following the leading of the Holy Spirit in the way they mentor others. Mentors are believers who take the time to have their daily devotions, talk to the Lord through prayer, meditate on Scripture, and listen to the response of the Lord through the Holy Spirit's guidance. Kinnaman points out that "Disciples cannot be mass-produced. Disciples are handmade, one relationship at a time."[42] For the church, this means the process of mentorship and discipleship takes time and cannot be rushed. If true spiritual growth is to happen, leaders must be patient and let mentoring happen organically by spending time with people just as Jesus' example teaches.

The issue according to Kinnaman is not whether young people are being discipled but rather how they are being discipled. He writes, "the church needs to reconsider how we make disciples."[43] From here, it is important to reinforce that effective discipleship involves the guidance of the Holy Spirit. Kinnaman proceeds to give six examples of how discipleship under the leading of the Holy Spirit should look. These six points are helpful not only in

39. Kinnaman, *You Lost Me*, 22.

40. Ibid., 22.

41. Ibid., 13.

42. Ibid.

43. Ibid., 201.

discipling young people, but also in assimilating new believers and people of all ages. Also the six points are helpful not only in discipling but also in mentoring our young people to be future leaders.

First, spiritual mentors need to allow the Holy Spirit to guide them from being overprotective to discernment. "Overprotectiveness discourages risk taking and uses fear to 'protect' the next generation. Discernment guides young people to trust God fearlessly and follow Christ in the power of the Spirit, even at the risk of their lives, reputations, and worldly success."[44] Kinnaman places the role of the Holy Spirit front and center in the ministry of mentoring. "Let's recognize that the Holy Spirit has plans for the next generation that are bigger than what they can dream for themselves, and let's make it our business to tune their hearts to hear his voice, not just ours."[45] This is a an appropriate posture to take in order to be clear that we are simply vessels used by God in partnership with what the Lord is doing in the lives of his people.

Second, spiritual mentors need to allow the Holy Spirit to guide them from a shallow faith to apprenticeship. "After more than a decade and a half of research into American faith, I believe that the Christian church in the United States has a shallow faith problem because we have a discipleship problem."[46] According to Kinnaman, the reason that the church in the United States has a shallow faith problem is because it is trying to mass-produce disciples, fails to provide meaningful rituals, expects too little from the next generation, and fixates on quantity of attendees over quality of those present.[47] As a whole, it is time for the Church to shift its focus back to Christ-centered values and for mature Christians to focus more on the relational aspect of connecting with people so that a more long lasting impact will develop through the process of mentorship and discipleship.

Third, spiritual mentors need to allow the Holy Spirit to guide them from being anti-science by "stewarding young people's

44. Ibid., 104.

45. Ibid., 105.

46. Ibid., 120.

47. Ibid., 120–25.

gifts and intellect."[48] Kinnaman notes that according to a Barna Group Youth Poll that was done in 2009, only one percent of youth pastors addressed a subject that was science related.[49] He goes on to say that "if only 1 out of 100 youth workers are talking about issues of science how can we possibly hope to prepare a generation to follow Jesus in our science-dominated culture?"[50] Many times, those who do talk about science, do so in such a negative light that young people are almost left feeling like they have to choose between God and science. However, there has to be another alternative than pitting science against God. "We need to develop young leaders who can capably serve in science, but not be so habituated to scientism that faith becomes untenable."[51] This requires mature Christian leaders to speak up and provide young leaders with a biblically grounded but scholastically balanced understanding of science that is compatible with their faith.

Fourth, spiritual mentors need to allow the Holy Spirit to guide them from a repressive form of sexual education, to one that is based on being relational. Young people should be discipled in how they view sex. Often, the church gives the viewpoint that the topic of sex is shameful, taboo, and not to be mentioned. On the other hand, the world has exploited the topic of sex and made it self-centered. A healthy discipleship includes a different viewpoint on the topic, "a deeper, more holistic, more Christ-filled ethic of sex."[52] That is, "rather than saying that *sex is taboo* (traditionalist) or that *sex is about me* (individualist), the relational approach to sexuality says, sex is good and it is about us."[53] This is a solid starting ground in order to launch into a healthy scripture based discussion about sex and God's intention of intimacy with his people.

48. Ibid., 206.
49. Ibid., 139–40.
50. Ibid., 140.
51. Ibid., 139.
52. Ibid., 160.
53. Ibid.

Fifth, spiritual mentors need to allow the Holy Spirit to guide them from one of exclusion to one of embrace.[54] Kinnaman asks the following questions: "How would the church be different if we were to reject exclusion as unacceptable and tolerance as not good enough? What would we do differently when discipling young adults to help them cultivate Christ-like empathy that identifies with the least, the last, and the lost?"[55] Discipling has to go from being exclusive towards those who are often labeled as "others," to embracing Scripture, practice of service, and empathy, especially with those who are considered the least of these. This aspect of discipleship is crucial because it involves embracing the practice of service. "Are we making service to the outsider a central component of discipleship?"[56] Discipleship is not well rounded and effective unless it has at its core service to others, which is the sixth and last aspect of effective discipleship. Going from doubting to doing, i.e. "faithfully work through doubts by doing acts of service with and for others."[57] This does not mean there is no room for doubt at all, but that serving others along side a mentor is a healthy way to work through and deal with doubts.

Kinnaman makes a very important and crucial point, i.e. discipleship in service should be based on giftedness. Under his second aspect of discipleship, or apprenticeship, one is to find "what young people are gifted for and called to do, and doing all we can to nurture that calling."[58] The Holy Spirit has given gifts to young people and a mentor is to help young people recognize the privilege and opportunity to use and nurture these gifts in service to others.

Spiritual giftedness then is recognized through discipleship. For example, in the *Seventh-day Adventist Believe* book, it explains the fundamental beliefs of the Seventh-day Adventist Church about Spiritual Gifts and how they are discovered. The book

54. Volf, *Exclusion and Embrace*.

55. Kinnaman, *You Lost Me*, 181.

56. Ibid., 182.

57. Ibid., 206.

58. Ibid., 128.

recommends that spiritual gifts are discovered by the spiritual preparation of prayer, humility, and putting away differences with others. It goes on to assert that spiritual gifts are also discovered by the study of the Scriptures, openness to the leading of the Holy Spirit, and recognition and confirmation from the community of the believers.[59] While all these parts are important in discovering one's spiritual gifts, a spiritual mentor who has been present in the life of the mentee is able to guide the mentee through the process of understanding spiritual gifts and discerning the Spirit as it pertains to the context of serving others.

The Holy Spirit in Transforming Neighborhoods

When the Holy Spirit gives spiritual gifts for service, it is to bless the communities that the Christian lives in. Timothy Keller stresses the importance of discipleship within the church for ministry in the world. "It is the responsibility of the ordained leadership to build up the church and its members through the ministry of the Word and sacraments. However, one critical focus of that ministry must now be the discipling of the laity for ministry in the world."[60] What Kinnaman stresses for the need of discipling young people, Keller stresses as a critical focus for all the members. Keller also states that if at least twenty to twenty-five percent of church members are discipled for ministry, "it creates a powerful dynamism that infuses the whole church and greatly extends the church's ability to edify and evangelize."[61] Just as Kinnaman notes, Keller also writes that this discipling of laity is not based on a cookie cutter model, but upon gifts.

> Only if we produce thousands of new church communities that regularly win secular people to Christ, seek the common good of the whole city (especially the poor), and disciple thousands of Christians to write plays,

59. Ministerial Association, *Seventh-day Adventists Believe*, 243–44.
60. Keller, *Center Church*, 277.
61. Ibid., 281.

> advance science, do creative journalism, begin effective and productive new businesses, use their money for others, and produce cutting-edge scholarship and literature will we actually be doing all the things the Bible tells us that Christians should be doing! This is how we will begin to see our cities comprehensively influenced for Christ.[62]

Keller notes that discipleship is to be done in many different ways, he gives examples of writing plays, advancing science, and journalism. Of course, these examples are based upon each person's gifts. This is why the presence of a mentor is very helpful in each mentee's life to use these gifts effectively for the up building of the Kingdom and discerning the Holy Spirit. Keller recognizes the work of the Holy Spirit in leading, choosing, organizing the church as it focuses on discipleship.[63] Everyone has a role to play in the divine story of God and humanity, future leaders are to be mentored in discipling and they in turn are to disciple individuals for service.

Keller's point is that Christians are to be a positive influence in the world. According to him, this is only possible if discipleship is central to the practice of the church. A part of discipleship is not only helping Christians to know their spiritual gifts, but also understanding the fruit of the Holy Spirit. "The Spirit of God sends God's people into the neighborhoods with his fruit. Christians can be the embodiment of peace if in fact they are full of the Spirit and peace and wholeness reside with them and through them as they go out with the message of peace."[64] The role of the Holy Spirit then in discipleship includes both spiritual gifts and spiritual fruit in order to impact the world for the kingdom of God.

There are many ways that Christianity has tried to impact the lives of individuals in the community. Some methods have been more successful than other methods. One method of impacting the community that has done more harm than good is the method

62. Ibid., 292.

63. Ibid., 346–47.

64. Boren, *Missional Small Groups*, 143.

of the Christian Right in trying to impact the communities of America through political changes. As the communities in America struggle with poverty, crime, and other challenges, Beverly LaHaye calls for action by the Christian community:

> The challenge stands before us. The question each of us must answer is this: Will I accept this challenge? . . . Christians can change our country . . . You and I have a tremendous opportunity to influence public policy in order to open the doors for the truth of the gospel to be communicated in all areas of our society . . . Today, the future of America hangs in the balance. It is up to you and me—the Christians throughout this great nation—to get on our knees and pray, educate ourselves, and mobilize the members of our churches to action. Our nation's future is at stake.[65]

James Davison Hunter explains how churches may impact the communities of America if they want to follow the methods of the Christian Right:

> For parishes and churches, the call to action means forming congregants through a process of political socialization. It is difficult to say how much this occurs in local churches or to what degree it is systematized when it does occur. For activists in this movement, the ideal church would be like the West County Assembly of God, a 600-member Evangelical congregation in Missouri. The church's pastor, John A. Wilson, gives sermons that extol the importance of opposing abortion, stem cell research, and same-sex marriage, and he publicly says he supported President Bush's decision to go to war in Iraq. To promote involvement in social issues, the church has a dozen-member "moral action team" that holds open meetings for parishioners each month. They inform church members about socially conservative electoral issues. They register them to vote at stands outside the sanctuary on designated "voter registration" Sundays.

65. LaHaye, "How Christians Make an Impact on Their Government."

> During elections, the "moral action team" even drives church members to the polls.[66]

According to the Christian Right, one major method of impacting the communities of America is through the right politicians pushing through the right policies. The authors of the book *Hijacked* share statistics that reveal a partisan shift in Evangelicals:

> Just before the passage of the 1965 Voting Rights Act, white evangelical Protestants self-identified as 68% Democrat, 25% Republican, and 7% Independent—making up a significant part of what was often referred to at the time as "the solid Democrat South . . ." In 1978, just two years before Reagan's election, 53% of white evangelical Protestants still identified with the Democratic Party, compared to 30% who identified with the Republican Party . . . The year 2008 is nearly an exact mirror image, with 54% identifying as Republican and 34% identifying as Democrat.[67]

Former Unites States House of Representative Tony Hall, explains some of the maneuvers of the Christian Right, also known as the Moral Majority. "When the Moral Majority was young and vibrant they used to publish the voting records. They would have ten votes every year, and if you did not vote eight out of ten votes with the Moral Majority they would say you were not a Christian."[68] Pressuring representatives to vote a certain way is one maneuver of the Moral Majority, otherwise they spread the news that the representative is not a Christian and needs to be voted out. Stephen Baldwin, speaking at Vaules Voter Summit, made the statement, "We are the hands of the Lord. I don't know about you, but I am putting some boxing gloves on mine."[69]

66. Hunter, *To Change the World*, 122.

67. Slaughter, *Hijacked*, 4, 5.

68. Ibid., 115.

69. In a statement made at the Values Voter Summit (Hilton Hotel, Washington, D.C., 12 September 2008). Quote taken from Hunter, *To Change the World*, 120.

As Christians, we are the hands of Jesus, but we are not to put on boxing gloves to transform our communities. Putting boxing gloves on our hands will hurt our influence in the world, not help it. Tony Hall explained well the negative impact of the Christian Right:

> I can't tell you in those days how many people came up to me who were Democrats or more liberal in their thinking who said that we know that you are a Christian but if those are the kind of people that are part of your faith we do not want any part of this stuff. In other words, they were really hurting the cause of Christ. They were getting so involved in politics that they were really hurting the cause of what God is all about.[70]

We are to have the Holy Spirit fill our hearts with the love of Jesus, then go into our communities as the hands of Jesus to bless, serve, and love our communities. And the best way to make this happen is to organize our churches into small groups based on passions and gifts, mentoring and discipling in following Jesus and listening to the leading of the Holy Spirit.

The authors of the book *Hijacked* propose that instead of trying to get the Christian churches to unite under political policies and certain political representatives, "allegiance to Christ is the only allegiance that is required to be a member of Christ's Body."[71] In chapter six of *Hijacked,* the authors propose three things that the churches may do in order to make a positive difference in the community.

First, Christ followers are to love one another, "Love transcends political and doctrinal ideologies. So we must put that love into practice in the church, demonstrating to the world that differences do not have to bring contention or division."[72] Ephesians 2:14–18 is quoted in support of this suggestion, and the role of the Holy Spirit is important in unity:

70. Slaughter, *Hijacked,* 115.

71. Ibid., 96.

72. Ibid., 99, 101.

> For He Himself is our peace, who made both groups into one and broke down the barrier of the dividing wall . . . And He came and preached peace to you who were far away, and peace to those who were near; for through Him we both have our access in one Spirit to the Father.[73]

Second, leaders in churches are to teach, that is to mentor and disciple in living, serving, and voting as Christ followers. "We must not underestimate the power of our leaders to guide the church as a witness for love in a contentious culture . . . We must learn how to participate in the political process while refusing to participate in demeaning, divisive partisanship."[74] And the third suggestion is to pursue the mind of Christ. "The community of Christ is called to pursue an alternative path from the political power structures of the world."[75] 1 Corinthians 2:13 is one of the Bible references used as a support for the third suggestion: "Which things we also speak, not in words taught by human wisdom, but in those taught by the Spirit."

According to the authors of *Hijacked,* the Holy Spirit is important as the church looks to positively impact the communities. In fact in the conclusion of the book, two references are made to the Holy Spirit's role in the mission of the church:

> We need the whole church to help us navigate the truth of God's word through the guidance of the present Holy Spirit for the accomplishment of Jesus' mission in the postmodern world . . . The church will need to develop a deeper theological understanding of the Holy Spirit as it relates to determining God's will in today's global context.[76]

Hunter makes the same point, that the world cannot be impacted by Christianity in a positive way unless Spirit led discipleship is central to Christian practice. According to Hunter, changing the world boils down to discipleship. Discipling Christians to be a

73. Ephesians 2:14, 17, 18.

74. Slaughter, *Hijacked*, 102, 103.

75. Ibid., 105.

76. Ibid., 126, 127.

positive presence in the neighborhoods and communities where they live. He writes:

> Beyond the worship of God and the proclamation of his word, the central ministry of the church is one of formation; of making disciples. Making disciples, however, is not just one more program—it is not Sunday School, a Wednesday night prayer meeting, or a new book one must read. Formation is about learning to live the alternative reality of the kingdom of God within the present world order faithfully. Formation, then, is fundamentally about changing lives.[77]

Changing the world by changing lives through discipleship is only possible when leaders recognize the working of the Holy Spirit in their own lives, the small groups that they lead, the church they attend, and the community in which they live. Missional small groups then need to have the conversation of "what the Spirit of God is doing in the world and through us as God's people."[78] If Christianity will make a difference in the world for the better, it will need to have the conversation and recognition of the work of the Holy Spirit both in the church and in the community.

Discipleship is the key for Kinnaman, Keller, and Hunter in making a difference in the lives of young people and in the world. But in order for discipleship to be effective, mentoring under the guidance of the Holy Spirit is essential. Mentors are to teach mentees that "what serves the discipleship of Jesus, and can be put to use there, comes from the Holy Spirit, and what comes from the Holy Spirit leads us along the way of Jesus Christ and into his discipleship. What the Synoptic Gospels call the discipleship of Jesus, the apostle Paul calls life in the Spirit."[79] Essentially then the leading of the Holy Spirit is necessary for discipleship no matter the age group being engaged.

In conclusion, a Christian should live life with the purpose of following Jesus Christ. While Christ is central to the Christian,

77. Hunter, *To Change the World*, 236–37.

78. Boren, *Missional Small Groups*, 25.

79. Moltmann, *The Source of Life*, 17.

we must remember that pneumatology is just as important as Christology. "The Spirit makes Christ present to believers, unites believers to Christ, spans the gap between there and here, then and now. When we talk about the Christian life, we are talking about the work of the Spirit, and vice versa."[80] In the current context, this is why more leaders are endeavoring to start up small groups with the focus of mentoring and discipling for spiritual growth and service. With this renewed awareness, the guidance of the Holy Spirit is being emphasized. Discipleship is important in the Christian life, therefore the church is in need of mentors who know how to lead in discipleship and also know how to mentor future mentors. In this way, mentees are able to learn how to lead and disciples learn how to identify their spiritual gifts of the Holy Spirit and learn to be guided by the presence of the Holy Spirit as they go out and impact the world for the Kingdom. In the next chapter, we will summarize key sources used in the foundations and how they apply to the project as well as look at the effectiveness of mentoring in the contemporary setting of education at the college level.

80. Inbody, *The Faith of the Christian Church*, 249.

Chapter 6

College Campuses and Mentoring

IN A CONTEMPORARY CONTEXT some nursing programs in colleges and universities are looking to mentoring programs to help first year students excel in their education. One such mentoring study conducted was the grant-funded Peer Mentor Tutor Program (PMTP) done for at-risk students in Appalachia. Students entering a nursing program face many challenges like, "include heavy course loads, difficult science core courses, and the failure to understand the commitment needed for success in the nursing major."[1]

Another challenge for the nursing students was the reality that many who "enrolled in nursing programs often work part-time or full-time and care for family members while contending with other personal responsibilities. These factors all have the potential to contribute to student attrition."[2] In order to try to help the first year nursing students, the Peer Mentor Tutor Program was implemented. "The goals of the program were to increase the retention rate of nursing students, especially during their first two semesters in nursing, and enhance the overall academic proficiency of both mentor-tutors and their mentees."[3]

1. Robinson, "A Peer Mentor Tutor Program," 286.
2. Ibid.
3. Ibid.

The structure of the program included twenty-one peer mentor-tutor groups, with ninety-seven at-risk students participating. There was a faculty advisor that was appointed to the program.

> The adviser was responsible for arranging mentor training sessions, reviewing students for inclusion into the program, tracking academic outcomes, organizing peer mentor-tutor materials, organizing scholarship incentives, enabling communication between peer mentor-tutors and nursing course coordinators, and providing mentorship for the peer mentor-tutors themselves.[4]

The peer mentor-tutor students that were selected, were students who had "earned As or Bs in PMTP courses and had a desire to participate in the program."[5] Mentor-tutors were trained to become mentors by the faculty advisor. The mentor-tutors committed to the program for one academic semester, they were to have a positive attitude, and "an understanding of the need to maintain confidentiality as they connected with peers on both a personal and professional level."[6]

The criteria for the participation of mentees were individuals who have either failed a previous nursing course, or a previous biological science course, students with a grade point average of 2.3 to 2.8 and were recommended by a nurse faculty member or advisor. The ratio of mentor-tutors to mentees was to be 1:5. The peer mentor-tutor groups were to meet weekly for two-hour sessions for the academic semester. "Sessions varied with regard to mentor-related and tutor-related activities. Most often the focus was on tutoring for successful course completion. A certain amount of time was spent on study strategies, test-taking skills, anxiety, stress reduction, and time management."[7]

When the study results came in for the 2007 PMTP program, 97 participants completed the PMTP, this represented a completion rate of eighty percent. "Of those students completing the

4. Ibid., 287.

5. Ibid.

6. Ibid.

7. Ibid., 287, 288.

program, seven students earned As, 46 earned Bs, and 36 earned Cs in courses receiving PMTP support. The remaining eight students were unsuccessful, even with participation in the PMTP."[8] According to the exam performance, "mentees earned significantly higher test scores throughout the year than the control group (mean score for mentees, 83.4 percent; for controls, 80 percent)."[9] In the pharmacology exam scores however there was no difference. "The authors note that students have historically struggled with pharmacology, and this has been an ongoing concern."[10]

The mentees did perform marginally better in psychiatric nursing than the control group. And the grade point average for the mentees was on the average a 2.80, compared to the control group GPA of 2.76. "In the first year of the PMTP, attrition rates did not change significantly when compared to previous years. However, an analysis showed that mentees accounted for less than 1 percent of the attrition from nursing courses."[11]

The program revealed some issues with peer mentoring. Some of the issues dealt with communication problems, delays in submitting documentation or evaluations and some mentors and mentees failing to honor their commitments. Two mentors resigned in the first program and some of the mentees stopped participating. But there were positive benefits to the peer mentor program. There was the benefit of at-risk students having support by their peers, then there was the benefit to the mentors as well, "four mentors reported that this experience sparked interest in a career in nursing education."[12]

Ashland University together with University of Akron also began a three-year longitudinal study on peer-to-peer mentoring for freshmen nursing students. The program is in its second year and a paper was written to show some of the results of the first year

8. Ibid., 288.

9. Ibid.

10. Ibid.

11. Ibid., 288, 289.

12. Ibid., 289.

of the program.[13] According to the program "mentoring is defined as a developmental relationship where an individual with more experience agrees to guide a less experienced person. Mentoring usually leads to mutual learning, dialog, and challenge, which become foundational to the relationship (Bozeman & Finney, 2007)."[14]

There were a total of 137 participants in the program, eighty-eight were mentors and forty-nine students were mentees. Since there were more mentors than mentees, several mentees received more than one mentor. The average age of the mentors was 22.5 and for the mentees was 18.5. Training was provided to the mentors in order to know how to support the mentees. The training consisted of a one-hour session where they received an "overview of the mentoring program, goals of the program, a review of university resources, and provision of a mentoring manual for quick access of information."[15]

The mentors were encouraged to meet with their mentees personally at least once a month. There were also some planned interventions on behalf of the University, three mentor-mentee events scheduled during the academic year, "one diversity educational session, an on-line community where mentees and mentors could participate in discussion boards."[16] After the conclusion of year one of the three-year study, not enough date was available for quantitative results, but some qualitative results were collected.

Students in the program were asked to respond to the following questions: "what has the peer mentoring program meant to you this year," and "please share any stories from your experience with the peer mentoring program." One theme that emerged from the responses was the theme of "connection and formed relationships." Here is one mentor's response:

> I really enjoyed the experience as a peer mentor. I was able to connect not only with my mentee, but also many

13. Clayburn, "Promoting Social Support."
14. Ibid.
15. Ibid.
16. Ibid.

> other underclassmen as well . . . the mentorship program allows everyone to connect and feel more comfortable . . . I was able to make new friends through the program that I may not have made otherwise (Junior nursing student mentor, 2013).[17]

Another mentor responded in the following words:

> I feel as though my participation had a positive influence on my mentee. Half way through the semester she knocked on my dorm door and asked me for some help on her anatomy homework; shortly after I learned she couldn't afford the book and therefore didn't have one, making homework and the class difficult. I fortunately kept mine from the previous year and let her borrow it for the rest of the semester and she was extremely grateful. Without the peer mentoring program this connection wouldn't have happened" (Sophomore nursing student mentor, 2013).[18]

Another theme that emerged was support, "especially through a mentee's difficult transition to college or in stressful life situations where the mentor gave support to the mentee, as illustrated by the following responses of a mentee and her mentor:"[19]

> She (the mentor) has been a blessing to me and been there when I needed her . . . she went through the nursing program the same way I am now (Advanced Entry program) . . . she reassured me . . . when I felt awkward and out of place . . . she assured me she knew how I was feeling and it was going to be ok. The mentor program really helped me get through my first year of school here" (Sophomore nursing student mentee, 2013).[20]

> "(My mentee) was going into the Advanced Entry program . . . I knew I had to get to know her and stay in touch . . . turns out we are alike and she is actually a

17. Ibid.
18. Ibid.
19. Ibid.
20. Ibid.

> younger version of myself! I continue to make sure to check in on her and make sure she's doing alright because I know how hard that first summer (of the program) was for me . . . I want to make sure she has someone to tell her it is doable . . . I've made my place open for her to come and get help studying whenever she needs. I hope . . . she'll join the program as a mentor and that she'll find someone to help go through the process the way I did" (Junior nursing student mentor, 2013).[21]

The results of the first year of the program were concluded in the following words: "Although quantitative results did not show significance in the area of increased support, the anecdotal qualitative themes are supportive of peer mentoring and show increased perceived support along with connection and formed relationships that will ideally continue to provide support to the mentees."[22] I have included two recent mentor related programs in the nursing field to show that mentoring is considered to be an option in Nursing Programs to help students adjust to college life, help them with their studies and to find them support.

There were others studies done in classroom settings that showed good results of mentoring. According to one study, "beneficial results included grade improvement and close mentor-mentee relations lasting over one year (Ramsey, Blowers, Merriman, Glenn, & Terry, 2000)."[23] Here are some results of a few other studies:

> Rodger and Trembaly (2003) studied the effects of peer mentoring for a population of freshman university students. Those students committed to the peer mentor program earned significantly higher final course grades than students in an equivalent control group; however, the study found little effect on retention from the freshman to the sophomore year. Higgins (2004) investigated the effects of peer tutoring on retention and academic improvement in a medical-surgical nursing course.

21. Ibid.

22. Ibid.

23. Robinson, "A Peer Mentor Tutor Program," 286.

> Providing peer tutoring to at-risk students helped decrease course attrition from 12 percent to 3 percent.[24]
>
> Penman and White (2006) focused on the importance of a mentoring relationship to support academically at-risk students. Evaluation revealed that mentorship for at-risk students improved motivation and chances for academic improvement. Sutherland, Hamilton, and Goodman (2007) evaluated a mentoring, tutoring, and advisement approach designed to increase program retention for at-risk, disadvantaged, minority students. Sixty-fours [sic] students were mentored using a faculty mentor model, and tutoring was provided by expert practitioners. Participants demonstrated improved retention to graduation and greater success on the NCLEX-RNâ.[25]

From numerous studies it has shown that one way to help students succeed in their studies is through mentoring. This may be applied to mentoring for new Christians in a local church setting. Many times a pastor or pastoral team is unable to give the support and help needed to all the members and new members that join the church. Just as peer mentors are helpful at University campuses, so member mentors would be beneficial to a local congregation. It is one way to find support, spiritual growth, and help needed for individual members.

24. Ibid.

25. Ibid.

Chapter 7

Mentoring in a Church Setting

Mentoring at the Mansfield Seventh-day Adventist Church

The Mansfield Seventh-day Adventist Church, located in Mansfield, Ohio is comprised of amazing, friendly, loving, grace-oriented Christians. It was a blessing for my wife, children, and I to live and serve in the church and community from the summer of 2009 to the beginning of 2015. I had the privilege to make the year of 2014, a year of mentoring and discipling through missional small groups. We began planning for the year of mentoring by having an assessment/planning group start meeting towards the end of 2013 to discuss, plan, and find ways to organize the church for mentoring and discipleship.

For the group assessment, seventeen individuals were chosen. These individuals were selected because they were leaders in the church, either members of the church board or leaders in certain church ministries. The group was comprised of eight husband and wife couples and one single person. The single person was in her twenties at the time, the next couple was in their thirties, the next four couples were in their forties, and the next two couples were in their fifties, with the last couple retired. Nine of the seventeen were in the health profession as doctors, nurse practitioners, a nurse and an instructor at a nursing school. Two brothers owned their own business, and as mentioned, a couple was retired.

Our first meeting took place November 9, 2013, with a fellowship meal after church service. Of the seventeen individuals invited, twelve were present. One question was asked to start the discussion: What do you think is the greatest challenge to the church? For many, the greatest challenge was lack of involvement framed in comments such as, "People are too busy to get involved," or "There is a lack of commitment or connectedness on the part of many members." Another person noted that there is a lack of invitation. Another person mentioned that the processing of becoming a member needs to be evaluated, for while people may join the church, involvement does not seem to increase. Another person expressed the concern that the youth of the church are being neglected. We finished the discussion with the proposal to ask for the Holy Spirit to lead us as we face these challenges and prepared to meet again in December.

Our next meeting was December 14, 2013, with ten of the seventeen members in attendance. The group met at the home of one of the couples in the group after church service. We reviewed the challenges of the church and confirmed that it was a lack of involvement due to lack of time, lack of commitment, lack of connectedness, including the youth being disconnected, and a lack of a good process in joining the church. We dialogued about ways to face these challenges and I proposed moving forward with missional small groups as a way to deal with the lack of involvement. All decided to move forward with missional small groups, and we discussed how this would look at the local level. We decided to meet again and to deliver sermons on educating the church about missional small groups. At this meeting we came up with sixteen possible missional small groups, with leaders and possible participants in each group.

The group met again on January 18, 2014, in our home, again right after church service. Fourteen of the seventeen individuals attended the meeting. We discussed what missional small groups look like, and the roles of the mentors in these small groups. We also discussed having a Sabbath where church members would have an opportunity to sign up for the missional groups proposed in our last meeting. On February 22, 2014, booths were set up in the narthex of the church so that after church service, people had an opportunity to see the different missional small groups that we named Life Groups[1] and to sign up for them.

The next meeting was on March 22, 2014. Again we met at the homes of one of the members in the group, with thirteen of the seventeen members present. This meeting was to discuss how their small groups were operating, if started, or what they would do to begin the small groups. We decided to meet every other month in order to continue the small groups and discuss their operation. I asked the participants to fill out two sheets. One sheet had information about their Life Groups, their mission verse, names of the participants, the number of times they will meet in the next three months, and the focus of their meeting. The second sheet was a covenant for the Life Group leaders to sign (See Appendix A).

We have also used the Ginghamsburg Church as an example, adopting some of their points for our Life Group leader's covenant. What we borrowed included a covenant of relationship with the local church, a promise to pray daily for the individuals in their Life Groups, a commitment to grow spiritually, to attend Life Group sessions for support and accountability, to mentor someone else and to contact the pastor when in need of help. What we omitted from the Ginghamsburg Life Group covenant was the semester months that the Life Group would run. We decided to allow the leaders to decide when to stop or start a small group without going through semester seasons.

The group met for the fifth time on May 31, 2014 in the home of one of the group members for fellowship meal and further discussion. Again we met after church service. Every group leader gave a report on how their Life Groups were starting to take shape,

1. Life Groups is the name used by the Ginghamsburg Church, 6759 S. County Rd. 25A, Tipp City, OH 45371. For more information about Ginghamsburg Church, you may visit their website www.ginghamsburg.org. We have decided to adopt the same name for our small groups.

if they were already meeting and how many were attending. Then we watched a video on Life Groups.

The group met for the last time on September 20, 2014, at the home of an elder. Fifteen of us were present on a beautiful Saturday afternoon. We met outside, and the meal and fellowship with the leaders was fantastic, our best meeting so far. One reason is that we had the energy of a new Life Group leader—a group that was not established at the onset. Her enthusiasm in having the opportunity to use her gifts and passions in service, as well as mentoring and discipling others in the process, was wonderful to see. The topic discussed was mentoring and discipling. We discussed Crow's definition of mentoring: "Empowering emerging leaders. A mature leader helps an emerging leader both clarify and implement God's call."[2] Then we discussed Crow's definition of discipling: "Helping new believers grow in Christ. A more mature believer helps a new believer grow in following Jesus."[3]

We talked about the differences and similarities between mentoring and discipling. Then we looked at Jesus' mentoring methodology based upon Crow's article and how it could apply to the Life Groups we set up. Each group leader gave an update of where they were with their Life Groups and their goals for the next three months. We finished our meeting with prayer and the decision to continue meeting for fellowship, support, and accountability.

From our five meetings together as a group, we realized the importance of mentoring and discipling in order for the church to make a difference in the lives of those attending and in the community. One recurring theme was the importance of mentoring and discipling young people, mentoring some young people for leadership and discipling all young people to be Christ followers. It was amazing to see the group come together in fellowship and turn from discussions on the larger church to becoming missional small group leaders. From the original seventeen individuals that began the group assessment, two have stopped coming, and we

2. Crow, "Multiplying Jesus Mentors," 36, 90.

3. Ibid.

have added one. The two that stopped coming felt they were not ready to lead a missional small group, and the individual that joined the group has created a missional small group on her own: The group has transformed into mentoring ground for missional small group leaders.

Field Experience

The field experience began in the beginning of January 2014, focusing on raising awareness of the importance of discipleship. The sermon series for the year was based on discipleship (Appendix B). In addition, it was coincidental or providential that the Sabbath School quarterly for the Seventh-day Adventist denomination was on discipleship for the first quarter of 2014.[4] Therefore, the elder who teaches the Sabbath School quarterly taught on discipleship every Saturday morning for Sabbath School from January through March.

After raising awareness on the importance of discipleship, the plan was to start missional small groups. We already had a few small groups in the church, a prayer group that met before church service Saturday morning for prayer, a men's basketball group that played every Tuesday night, and a women's group that gathered for Bible study or social events. Other than the prayer group leader, each small group leader was part of the original group assessment. They were being mentored now to transform the groups into missional small groups. As a reminder, it is Boren's three missional rhythms, that defined for us a missional small group: The rhythm of communion with God, the rhythm of relating to one another, and the rhythm of engaging the neighborhood.[5]

Each Life Group leader was encouraged to invite individuals to join their Life Groups. On February 22, 2014, the narthex of the church was set up with different themed Life Group booths. The sermon that day was based on chapter seven of McDonald's book

4. Solis, *Discipleship*.

5. Boren, *Missional Small Groups*.

The Disciple Making Church. As Paul received his Macedonian call, so the Holy Spirit has a Macedonian call for each of us, a call to service. With that we concluded the service with a hymn and prayer, encouraging individuals to visit each booth and pray about the call of service that God is giving them.

Each booth was a potential Life Group that would be led by those who were part of the group assessment. Each leader had a passion and gift in the area that they chose. The County Fair Evangelism Life Group engaged the community by offering encouraging Bible study lessons, health lessons, and other materials at the county fair. The Koinonia Youth Life Group concentrated on mentoring and discipling the young people in the church through social gatherings and Bible study and chose Hebrews 10:24, 25 as their Life Group Bible verse: "And let us consider how to stimulate one another to love and good deeds, not forsaking our own assembling together, as is the habit of some, but encouraging one another; and all the more as you see the day drawing near." The deaconesses and deacons Life Groups would concentrate on making sure the church building was well maintained and that the church edifice itself would speak to the mission of the church, that of loving God, loving one another, and loving the community. Grace Place is the Life Group that would serve those in the community that had needs such as clothing or food. Grace Place chose Titus 2:11 as their Life Group verse: "For the grace of God has appeared, bringing salvation to all" (NRSV). Habitat Group would join Habitat for Humanity in building homes or renovating homes. The Habitat Group chose Matthew 13:55 as their Bible verse: "Is not this the carpenter's son? Is not His mother called Mary, and His brothers, James and Joseph and Simon and Judas?" Ladies of Legacy is the Life Group for women to fellowship and study Scripture together. Ladies of Legacy chose Ecclesiastes 4:9–10: "Two are better than one, because they have a good reward for their toil. For if they fall, one will lift up the other; but woe to one who is alone and falls and does not have another to help" (NRSV). The Mansfield Seventh-day Adventist Elementary School Boosters is comprised of our church school board members. The purpose is to continue to challenge this group to become missional in how the church school operates. The Mansfield Seventh-day Adventist Elementary School Boosters chose Proverbs 22:6: "Train children in the right way, and when old, they will not stray" (NRSV). Men's Basketball is the Life Group for men who love to play basketball. The Family Bible Study, are Life Groups started in the homes of members with the purpose of studying Scripture together. We have two families who have opened up their homes and started Life Groups with emphasis on Bible study. They are also encouraged to include loving the community, with the emphasis of communing with God and relating to one another. Praise Team is the Life Group that serves the church every weekend with worship in music and are encouraged to engage the community with their musical talents. The Praise Team chose Psalm 47:6, 7: "Sing praises to God, sing praises; sing praises to our King, sing praises. For God is the King of all the earth; sing praises with a skillful psalm." Finally, the Prayer Group is the Life Group that meets before church service and prays for the prayer requests brought before the church, for the community, and for the suffering around the world.

Each group is different from the other, yet all the Life Groups are to practice the three missional rhythms as defined by Boren: loving God, loving one another, and loving the community. The leaders were mentored on these three practices, as well as on praying daily for those who joined their Life Groups. In addition to the twelve Life Groups presented to the church on February 22, 2014, we also offered the opportunity for anyone to start a Life Group. One individual did start a Life Group called "Busy Bodies." This Life Group serves the community by sewing, knitting, making scarves, blankets, and clothing for individuals in the community and beyond. The Busy Bodies chose Ephesians 4:11–13 as their Bible verse, "And He gave some as apostles, and some as prophets, and some as evangelists, and some as pastors and teachers, for the equipping of the saints for the work of service, to the building up of the body of Christ; until we all attain to the unity of the faith, and of the knowledge of the Son of God, to a mature man, to the measure of the stature which belongs to the fullness of Christ."

Even though the Life Group leaders had already individually approached individuals to sign up for Life Groups, we still had additional people sign up for Life Groups. Two more signed up to be part of the County Fair. Six people signed up to be part of Grace Place. Three people signed up for the Habitat Group. One person signed up to join one of the in-home Bible study groups. Two people signed up for the Prayer Group, and three individuals signed up to potentially start a new Life Group. Of the three that signed up to start a new Life Group, Busy Bodies was the one that organized as a new Life Group because the group already had a clear leader who already started asking others to help with sewing projects.

After the February 22, 2014 Sabbath, I continued to meet with the group that started out as group assessment but became the group of Life Group leaders. We met March 22, 2014; May 31, 2014; and September 20, 2014. The details of those meetings were recorded earlier in the chapter. The focus of each meeting was to support each Life Group, ask questions of accountability, and continue to mentor the Life Group leaders. The mentoring included reminding the leaders to continue to pray for the Life Group members, to pray about mentoring one or two individuals in their groups for future potential leaders, and to disciple each Life Group member in loving God, loving one another, and loving the community.

Results

Each Life Group leader has worked hard in living missionally through the small groups, yet each Life Group was unique in how they went about being missional. Most of the Life Groups did not meet during the summer, but the County Fair Life Group worked hard during the summer setting up booths at the Richland County Fair and the Loudonville County Fair. They spoke to many people about Christ and handed out Bibles and Bible lessons to individuals. Koinonia has two leaders that have a passion for young people. They have gathered the names of fifty-five young people that they are praying for and have also met a few times for socializing. This is a good beginning for Koinonia, because youth ministry has virtually been non-existent for many years in the church.

Deacons and Deaconesses Life Groups have twelve projects that they would like to complete in the next couple of years to make the church building more welcoming and to reflect the missional theme of the church. Some of these projects include building a larger kitchen that would be used for missional purposes, remodeling the narthex in order for visitors and every member to be reminded weekly that we are the hands and feet of Jesus. They have done a good job inviting individuals to participate in the projects and involving people who have not been asked to serve for a number of years.

Grace Place has continued to serve the hungry once a quarter on Sabbath afternoons in Mansfield. Habitat Group came together on October 26 for a project in the community. The Mansfield Seventh-day Adventist Elementary School Boosters is also thinking of ways to have the young people be the hands and the feet of Jesus in the community. Joining the Habitat Group is just one of the ways they are being missional.

Ladies of Legacy continues to meet in restaurants for socializing. They begin with a devotional thought, spend time fellowshipping together, looking at the needs of women in the church and in the community and organizing to meet those needs. For example, if a young woman gives birth, they plan a baby shower for her, or if someone they know had a surgery or a loss of a loved one, Ladies of Legacy organizes to provide meals for the family. The group is very good in looking for ways to be the hands and the feet of Jesus to individuals in the church and in the community.

The Men's Basketball group has taken a break over the summer, but members of the group are anxious to pick up again after the kitchen is finished with remodeling. Before the summer break, the Men's Basketball Life Group looked for ways to adopt Boren's three missional rhythms. The Men's Basketball Life Group has evolved from just playing basketball to becoming missional. In order to practice the missional rhythm of communing with God, the group begins basketball with prayer. Before we pray, the offer is made to share prayer requests. Many open up about health concerns, family needs, works situations, and we pray for each request. We then practice relating to one another in love by positive remarks during basketball games instead of trash talking. Instead of intimidating the opponent on the other team with put downs, we strive to encourage one another with statements like, "Nice shot," "Good block," "Awesome rebound." Between games, we talk with one another about work, family, and spiritual themes. These are great opportunities to share with one another and deepen friendships. As for the rhythm of engaging the community, it is not hard to fill a basketball court with men in order to exercise. We use the opportunity to invite men to worship or other church events. One individual is studying for baptism because of the Men's Basketball Life Group. His wife is a member of the church, and he would not come to church when she invited him. He mentioned that he did not know anyone at church and felt uncomfortable coming to church, but after fellowshipping with church members on the basketball court and being invited to church, he felt comfortable coming to church and decided to give his life to Jesus. We have also examined other ways of engaging the community. For example, when one of the men and his wife had a baby, we congratulated him on the birth of his baby. In these ways the Men's Basketball Life Group looks beyond Tuesday night basketball and ministers to men who come to play basketball.

The in-home Bible study groups also took a break over the summer. As they started up this fall, they were encouraged to add loving the community to their fellowship. At this time, no results have been received on ways that they have engaged the community, but they are praying for ways to serve the community. The Prayer Life Group continues to meet Saturday mornings before church service to pray for the church service, the church leaders, the church members, and the community. With the prayer ministry, we have started praying through the church membership list, encouraging individuals not only to pray for church members, but also to send encouraging notes to one another. Church members have been blessed by receiving notes of encouragement from one another and by praying for one another. As was stated earlier, about two-thirds of the church members do not attend church. Thus, praying for the church members and sending encouraging notes to them is part of the mission of the church. The Praise Team has also been encouraged to use their gifts of music for the community. They served for a Women's Retreat for the Ohio Conference of Seventh-day Adventist in September 2014, and one future plan includes singing in nursing homes.

The last group, the Busy Bodies Life Group, has organized effectively to engage the neighborhood with sewing, knitting, and crocheting. They have provided dresses, blankets, scarves, dog toys, dolls, and doll clothing to different organizations locally and internationally. Some of the organizations they have served include Ontario Free Clothes Closet, Richland County Dog Pound, Richland Pregnancy Services, Richland County Crisis Pregnancy's Baby Boutique, Pump House Ministries of Ashland, Clothing to Ukraine, Coastal Adventist Churches of Kenya, Southern Luzon Mission in Phillipines, and Women's Clothing Mission of Mansfield. A card arrived to the church on October 11, 2014 from the Richland Pregnancy Services, with a note saying, "Thank you for the beautiful items created for our boutique. The ladies wanted me to let you know that the prototype of the changing pad, diaper, wipe packet went out the first day. They loved it! Again 'thank you' for blessing others with the talent God has given you." Again, another thank you card came in the mail on October 18, 2014 from the Richland Pregnancy Services. In the thank you card, the following note was written: "Dear 'Busy Bodies,' We are so appreciative of all the items that you create for our boutique. Thank for being the hands and feet of Christ in reaching out to these young moms in their time of need." These two notes demonstrate that the Busy Bodies Life Group understands what it means to be missional.

The results of the Life Groups have been positive in the church and in the community. Nine individuals were interviewed from the church after the project of mentoring, discipling, and serving through the Life Groups was well on its way. The first person interviewed said that she was very thankful for the Life Groups. She had felt that there was not much fellowship in the church, but through the Life Groups, she could fellowship with individuals on a more meaningful level, while at the same time using her gifts in blessing others. She said that in the past, equipping the saints from Ephesians 4:12 had always meant to be equipped in giving Bible studies and knowing the Bible, but now she understands that equipping the saints could also be done with fabric, thread, buttons, and clothing.

Another individual interviewed still feels that very little change has been made in the church. This individual was not present when Life Groups were launched on February 22, 2014, or invited by any of the Life Group leaders to participate. One area of growth for the project is that of sharing multiple times the different Life Groups that individuals could sign up for. The third individual that was interviewed said that he has learned more about mentoring and also realized that he has been mentoring people all along without even realizing it. He has spent much time mentoring his children and in mentoring individuals at the work place. He also feels that the project has helped move the church in the right direction, the direction of discipling and mentoring. The fourth individual interviewed mentioned that while we are moving in the right direction with mentoring and discipling, we need to do a better job with children's ministries and youth ministries, two groups that need a whole lot more support from the church. He also mentioned that we need to be careful of not turning Life Groups into just another program to keep church members busy, but that we allow the Holy Spirit to lead each Life Group and not force them to be a certain way just to keep members busy doing something.

The fifth individual interviewed felt that young people are still being neglected. While she is part of Koinonia, she believes that the Life Group still needs to do more to mentor and disciple young people. In interviewing her, it was evident that young people were her passion. The next two individuals, a husband and wife team, were interviewed together. They felt that awareness for discipleship has been raised in the church, but that meaningful change will take time. Moving from a traditional view of the church to a missional church will not happen quickly. Life Group leaders need to be motivated to continue mentoring, discipling, and serving. We need to spend time concentrating on the current Life Groups and encouraging the Life Groups to be missional. Again, the topic of mentoring young people and children came up. This theme of mentoring young people has surfaced many times in the group assessment as well as the interviews.

The eighth person interviewed felt that the project of missional small groups has been a tremendous blessing to the church. He has been involved in the Deacons and Deaconesses Life Groups and has seen many people involved in service in the last six to nine months that have not been involved in the nine years that he has been in the church. The last individual interviewed shared how living missionally has blessed her life recently. She was eating lunch one day with a friend from church at Olive Garden, where heard of an Olive Garden promotion that included forty-nine meals for one hundred dollars.[6] They asked the manager of Olive Garden if they could purchase the promotion in order to give the meals to individuals in need. The manager told them that they had sold out of the promotion but that he would be willing to be part of this project for free. The church member interviewed then started to pick up the meals every day and pray for the Holy Spirit to lead her to individuals in need of a meal. She realized that the task was too great for her to continue for forty-nine days, so she involved the Life Group "Ladies of Legacy" to help her in the project. After talking to her about her project of sharing Olive Garden meals with people in need, it became clear that she was thinking missionally while eating at Olive Garden, that she was relying on the leading of the Holy Spirit, and that she included a Life Group in serving the community.

6. The Italian Restaurant, Olive Garden, had a promotion in the fall of 2014, giving away a meal a day for the next forty-nine days for $100.00.

Reflections, Summary, Conclusion

After spending two years on the topics of mentoring, discipling, and service. I have grown personally in my understanding of each of these three themes. I have come to the conclusion that mentoring and discipling are not the same, that while all are called to be Christ followers and in need of discipling, some are to be mentored in order to lead and disciple. I also understood more clearly that it was the mentoring of individuals in my life that brought me to being a pastor in service for the Lord, that mentors are very important in our becoming and being disciples of Jesus Christ. Mentors are needed to help us grow in Christ, learn to discern the leading of the Holy Spirit, and helpful in leading us into service, into being the hands and feet of Jesus in the neighborhood.

Studying the stories of Elijah mentoring Elisha, Jesus mentoring Peter, and James White mentoring John Nevins Andrews, I have come to the conclusion that if the MSDA will make a difference in Mansfield, or if a church will make a difference in the community, then spiritual leaders will mentor and disciple members to follow Christ into the community through loving acts of service.

The plan in 2014 at the Mansfield Seventh-day Adventist Church was to mentor and disciple. We decided to do this through missional small groups that we named Life Groups. We were able to effectively raise awareness in the church of the need for discipleship, for being the hands and the feet of Jesus. We were able to transform some current small groups into missional small groups, as well as to create other missional small groups. It is too early to assess solid results from these Life Groups, yet positive feedback has come back already that shows that we are involving more members in service. We have seen more intention in coming together in small groups to commune with God, to relate to one another in love, and to serve the community. Clearly there are benefits that come with churches starting up missional small groups in order to mentor, disciple, and serve the community, but there are challenges that come with the project.

One of the challenges is the realization that it will take time to mentor individuals for leadership and discipleship. People that have been used to having church a certain way will take time to think differently about church and about mission. To shift the paradigm from having the pastor initiate and be involved in every ministry, to having church members start up and lead ministries takes time. Repetition, patience, and explanation are essential in helping people understand the benefits and the meaning of living as Christ followers in the community. It took us repeating numerous times over a period of months for people to start understanding the meaning of Life Groups, and even today there are some members who still have not tuned into what Life Groups are.

Another challenge comes with having to change some of the structures of the church in order to free up people to lead Life Groups. We were fortunate at MSDA that some of the structures of organization had been simplified already, but there will always be resistance to change by some people. Patience and teaching again and again the importance of following Jesus into the neighborhood has to be done to help individuals through the process of transition.

The third challenge is to find potential leaders of small groups that have time to be mentored and to run small groups. People are busy with the demands of having careers and with spending time with family. In the SDA church, only the pastor is a paid employee: everyone else is a volunteer. Sometimes the janitorial work is paid, but for many churches, that also is done on a volunteer basis. The challenge of having volunteers give so much of their time to being mentored, and then in turn mentoring, discipling, and serving through missional small groups is real. That is why it is important to allow each Life Group to chose when they meet, how often they meet, and how they choose to mentor, disciple, and serve, based upon the availabilities of the leaders and members of the groups.

A fourth challenge is to help the church realize that moving towards missional small groups will not grow the church fast numerically. What it will do is help those that are attending grow in their walk with Christ and in their service in the community.

Too often when the church does not see numerical results right away, they give up on a project. But mentoring and discipleship take time. Elijah spent time mentoring Elisha, Jesus spent time mentoring Peter and the other disciples, and James White spent time mentoring John Andrews. Building meaningful and lasting relationships takes time, but through the efforts of mentoring and discipleship come great benefits of healthy congregations growing in Christ and engaging the neighborhood.

There are still many areas in which we could improve and grow in. I acknowledge that starting up missional small groups takes time and much mentoring. I have learned that instead of having the booths for one weekend before the church, it would be good to leave the booths up for multiple weekends. Even after launching Life Groups, it is important to continue highlighting one of the Life Groups every week in order to keep in front of the church the opportunities for participation.

One growing edge for us locally has to do with our young people. Even though one of our Life Groups deals with mentoring and discipling young people, we need to do a better job supporting and helping this Life Group continue to grow and flourish. While some Life Groups will come to an end at some time, mentoring and discipling young people has to continue. Young people need to be involved in service and discipleship for the current health of the church and not only for its future. Churches have to make sure that as they are starting up missional small groups, they include individuals of all ages, especially young people.

In conclusion, this project may be a beneficial resource in a couple of ways for churches. First, churches that do not have missional small groups, may benefit from this project in learning how to start up small groups that concentrate not only on fellowship and Bible study but on being the hands and feet of Jesus. Another way that churches could benefit from this project is in mentoring young people. Mentoring and discipling are very important in spiritual growth and leadership, therefore young people are in need of Spirit led mentors. This project will give mentors biblical, historical, theological, and contemporary examples of mentoring, as well as an example of a project in mentoring.

Because of the project, more members started being involved in service in the church and in the community. They are involved because of mentoring and discipling through missional small groups. As a church we will continue to advocate for Boren's three rhythms of missional small groups: the rhythm of communion with God, the rhythm of relating to one another as a group on a deeper, more meaningful, loving manner, and the rhythm of engaging the neighborhood. This model has blessed individuals both in our church and in the community. I hope to see more individuals become leaders through mentoring, growing in Christ through discipleship, and being the hands and feet of Jesus in the community.

Chapter 8

Mentoring in Youth Ministry

Jesus Doing Youth Ministry

JESUS LOVED PARTICIPATING IN youth ministry. First he chose mostly young adults to mentor as his disciples. Then, he also stood up for and even elevated children to great importance in God's kingdom.

> At that time the disciples came to Jesus and said, "Who then is greatest in the kingdom of heaven?" And He called a child to Himself and set him before them, and said, "Truly I say to you, unless you are converted and become like children, you will not enter the kingdom of heaven. And whoever then humbles himself as this child, he is the greatest in the kingdom of heaven. And whoever receives one such child in My name receives Me; but whoever causes one of these little ones who believe in Me to stumble, it would be better for him to have a heavy millstone hung around his neck, and to be drowned in the depth of the sea.[1]

Jesus clarifies a number of points regarding children in this one story. First, he places a child in front of everyone and tells his

1. Matthew 18:1–6.

audience that there is much to learn from the humility of children. Then, Jesus gives the invitation to receive children in his name. Afterwards, Jesus warns his audience not to harm, hurt, or place a stumbling block in front of children. Children desire to come to Jesus, love to sing about him, talk to him, follow him, and we are not to stand between Jesus and the children. At one time, the disciples of Jesus stood between children and Jesus, and he confronted them for their mistake.

> And they were bringing even their babies to Him so that He would touch them, but when the disciples saw it, they began rebuking them. But Jesus called for them, saying, "Permit the children to come to Me, and do not hinder them, for the kingdom of God belongs to such as these. Truly I say to you, whoever does not receive the kingdom of God like a child will not enter it at all."[2]

Barnabas, the Great Mentor of the Early Church

Jesus was serious about welcoming children and mentoring young adults. One individual who followed in Jesus' footsteps and was truly a great mentor in the early church was Barnabas. Glenn McDonald, in his book *The Disciple Making Church* writes a whole chapter on Barnabas as a mentor.[3] McDonald notes that Acts 4:36 gives the name Barnabas the meaning of "Son of Encouragement."[4] And Barnabas lived up to that name, he was truly an encourager. Luke tells us in Acts 11:23 that when Barnabas visited the church at Antioch, "he rejoiced and began to encourage them all with resolute heart to remain true to the Lord; for he was a good man, and full of the Holy Spirit and of faith."[5] Barnabas was a great encourager because first of all he was a good man, who received the fullness of the Holy Spirit by accepting Christ's invitation: "If

2. Luke 18:15–17.
3. McDonald, *The Disciple Making Church*, 57–71.
4. Ibid., 61.
5. Acts 11:23, 24.

you then, being evil, know how to give good gifts to your children, how much more will your heavenly Father give the Holy Spirit to those who ask Him?"[6] Prayer, faith, goodness, were attributes that Barnabas possessed, and because of these attributes, he was an effective encourager of churches and young people.

McDonald also points out that as an encourager, Barnabas took risks in mentoring young people that others were too nervous to approach.[7] Luke records Acts 9:26, 27 what happened when Paul, three years after his conversion, goes to Jerusalem to meet the disciples of Jesus.

> When he [Paul] came to Jerusalem, he was trying to associate with the disciples; but they were all afraid of him, not believing that he was a disciple. But Barnabas took hold of him and brought him to the apostles and described to them how he had seen the Lord on the road, and that He had talked to him, and how at Damascus he had spoken out boldly in the name of Jesus."

The disciples at Jerusalem did all they could to ignore, reject, and made sure to avoid Paul. Barnabas on the other hand, takes the time to inform himself of the facts, and take a risk on befriending Paul, introducing him to the believers, and a few years later invite Paul to join the team of outreach at Antioch.

> And he [Barnabas] left for Tarsus to look for Saul [that is Paul]; and when he had found him, he brought him to Antioch. And for an entire year they met with the church and taught considerable numbers; and the disciples were first called Christians in Antioch.[8]

As Barnabas and Paul serve together at Antioch, the Holy Spirit tells the leaders of the church in Antioch to send Barnabas and Paul off for a missionary journey.

> While they were ministering to the Lord and fasting, the Holy Spirit said, "Set apart for Me Barnabas and Saul for

6. Luke 11:13
7. Ibid., 61.
8. Acts 11:25, 26.

> the work to which I have called them." Then, when they had fasted and prayed and laid their hands on them, they sent them away.[9]

McDonald brings out the point that Barnabas as a great mentor, started out as the leader of the trip, but then let Paul start taking on more of a leadership role.

> Bible scholars suggest that there is something to be learned from the progression of Luke's name ordering for these two men. Sequences are rarely arbitrary. At the beginning of their first missionary journey, it's "Barnabas and Saul" (Acts 13:7). By the end of the trip, however, Paul has apparently assumed the mantle of leadership from his mentor, as seen in "Saul and Barnabas (Acts 13:43, 46, 50). The adoring pagans of Lystra, however, trying to pin down the apparent mythological identities of the pair, decide that Barnabas must be Zeus, the king of the gods, while the chatty Paul must be his trusty sidekick Hermes, the messenger of Olympus (14:12). The church in Antioch increasingly saw Paul as the leader ("Paul and Barnabas" in 15:2) while in Jerusalem never doubted the seniority of the man they had known much longer ("Barnabas and Paul" in 15:12, 25).[10]

This type of mentoring by Barnabas, where the leader starts out leading, but then starts giving more of a leadership role to the mentee, could be applied in a practical sense in youth mentoring today by the following sequence of statements:

- I do and you watch.
- I do and you help.
- You do and I help.
- You do and I watch.
- You and I both repeat this pattern with someone else.[11]

9. Acts 13:2, 3.
10. McDonald, *The Disciple Making Church*, 62.
11. McDonald, *The Disciple Making Church*, 65.

Paul and Barnabas did go on to mentor others after their missionary journey, but it came because of a disagreement. Luke lays out the story in the following verses:

> After some days Paul said to Barnabas, "Let us return and visit the brethren in every city in which we proclaimed the word of the Lord, and see how they are." Barnabas wanted to take John, called Mark, along with them also. But Paul kept insisting that they should not take him along who had deserted them in Pamphylia and had not gone with them to the work. And there occurred such a sharp disagreement that they separated from one another, and Barnabas took Mark with him and sailed away to Cyprus. But Paul chose Silas and left, being committed by the brethren to the grace of the Lord. And he was traveling through Syria and Cilicia, strengthening the churches. Paul came also to Derbe and to Lystra. And a disciple was there, name Timothy, the son of a Jewish woman who was a believer, but his father was a Greek, and he was well spoken of by the brethren who were in Lystra and Iconium. Paul wanted this man to go with him; and he took him and circumcised him because of the Jews who were in those parts, for they all knew that his father was a Greek.[12]

Paul suggests to Barnabas to go back and revisit the believers and while Barnabas thinks it's a good idea, he wants to give another chance to John Mark to join the journey. John Mark, a cousin of Barnabas, partway into the first journey, gave up for some reason and abandoned Paul and Barnabas. Whether he became ill, tired of the hard journey, or missed his mother's home cooked meals with warm milk and fresh cookies, we don't know. But for Paul, John Mark was a disturbance, and it was strike one, you're out! For Barnabas, he was not ready to give up on Mark. Remember, Barnabas was "the Son of Encouragement" (Acts 4:36). Barnabas was also "a good man, and full of the Holy Spirit and of faith" (Acts 11:24). Just as he took a risk on mentoring Paul, he was not ready to give up on Mark. Barnabas was ready to continue encouraging,

12. Acts 15:36–16:3.

helping, mentoring, praying for, and praying with Mark. And Barnabas was ready to defend and stand up for Mark even if it meant letting Paul go on without him.

Paul, went on to mentor Timothy and Barnabas went on to mentor Mark. Yet, even though the disagreement was sharp between Paul and Barnabas, McDonald notes that "Paul's evident respect for his mentor [Barnabas] can still be found in his later writings (*Note* 1 Cor. 9:6).[13] Disagreements may take place in mentoring and may even lead the mentee to move on and start mentoring others. Yet respect for each other ought to continue, there is no room for negativity, put downs, and slanders. A continuation of encouragement should be fostered under the leading of the Holy Spirit.

Paul, towards the end of his ministry came to appreciate the fact that Barnabas did not give up on Mark. Writing to Timothy, his mentee, Paul says: "Only Luke is with me. Pick up Mark and bring him with you, for he is useful to me for service."[14] In humility, Paul recognizes that Mark has become a great servant of the Lord in the ministry. Thus, Paul could thank Barnabas for mentoring him, and Mark also could thank Barnabas for mentoring and standing up for him.

What we need in Christianity today is great mentors like Barnabas. What our churches are in need of, are great mentors like Barnabas. We are to pray to be mentors like Barnabas. Jesus' invitation of Luke 11:13 is for us also, to pray for the outpouring and infilling of the Holy Spirit. The Holy Spirit will fill our hearts with the goodness of Jesus, with faith, love, and encouragement for children, youth, and young adults. The Holy Spirit will lead us to be mentors like Barnabas.

13. McDonald, *The Disciple Making Church*, 62.

14. 2 Timothy 4:11.

Youth Ministry in the Ohio Conference of Seventh-day Adventists

I have the privilege and honor in serving the children, youth, and young adults in Ohio through programs such as Adventurers (a program designed for ages 6–9)[15], Pathfinders (designed for ages 10–15)[16], summer camp at Camp Mohaven, located just outside Danville, Ohio. Summer camp is a dynamic ministry, through which children from ages six to seventeen have the privilege to come and enjoy God's beautiful nature. Camp Mohaven offers swimming, canoeing, kayaking, water skiing, horseback riding, outdoor sports, rock climbing, high ropes and low ropes, archery, and many other fantastic events such banquets, the passion play, and morning and evening worship. The purpose of summer camp again is to be missional, hence summer camp becomes "Missional Mohaven."

Summer camp at Mohaven is missional two ways. First, summer camp is missional because the counselors and staff are mentored during staff week on deepening their relationship with Christ. As draw closer to Jesus, they are mentored to become the hands and feet of Jesus to the children that come to summer camp. Second, we pray and strive for making summer camp at Mohaven a trailer of heaven.[17] Often when we talk of trailer, we think of movie trailers. Well, we are not talking about movies, we are talking about heaven. We pray to make summer camp at Mohaven to be a powerful, dynamic, and a real trailer of what heaven and the new earth will be like. Where through nature, worship, love, kindness, and service we experience the presence of Christ through the Holy Spirit. That after spending a week at Mohaven, children and youth may go home saying; "if heaven is as joyful, fun, full of kind and loving individuals as the staff at Mohaven, who value

15. For more information about the Adventurers Program, visit: http://gcyouthministries.org/Ministries/Adventurers.

16. For more information regarding the Pathfinder Program, visit http://gcyouthministries.org/Ministries/Pathfinders.

17. The idea of missional being a trailer of heaven is taken from Michael Frost, *The Road to Missional*, 2011.

and respect each person, then we want to be in heaven and bring our friends with us." We desire not only to give a trailer of heaven but to send home missional children and youth who learn to share Christ through service, kindness, and love with their friends and families.

At Camp Mohaven we also host weekend retreats for middle school students, high school students, and young adults. Our middle school retreats are geared with the challenges and temptations that the students face daily at school, home, and their communities. Boys come to Mohaven at a different weekend than the girls, knowing that while girls and boys may have some of the same challenges, it is better to mentor them separately.

Our yearly high school retreat at Camp Mohaven is called "Live It Out." The purpose of the weekend is to learn how God's Word may be put into practice and lived out in the daily life. Again the focus is missional and oriented around God's Word. For young adults we have a yearly retreat called "Immersion." We strive to immerse young adults in God's Word for the purpose of becoming the hands and the feet of Jesus.

We also plan mission trips in Ohio, and other parts of United States, as well as overseas in order to give opportunities to young people to be the hands and feet of Jesus. Therefore there is much mentoring that is designed into each of these programs and events. And as has been discussed in previous chapters, effective mentoring is to be missional in nature and focus. In every program and event, missional mentoring is to be encouraged and practiced in some form.

Another way we strive to accomplish missional mentoring in Ohio is through the mentoring of leaders that work with children, youth, and young adults. We have organized the state of Ohio into eight regions and plan a yearly training for youth leaders of each region. The training is a one day evening, capped off with a social event for the youth and young adults of the particular region. This way we mentor and encourage building relationships between leaders and young people of the churches. Part of the focus is also to unite in being missional together. Some smaller churches may have three or four young people, but by uniting with other churches, together they may make a great impact for the kingdom of God.

It is so powerful when youth and young adults come together for the purpose of being the hands and feet of Jesus in some way within their region. We focus on mentoring youth leaders that they may mentor the children, youth, and young adults in their churches, and in turn the youth may become mentors of their peers. Just as Paul mentored Timothy and encouraged Timothy to go and mentor others. "You therefore, my son, be strong in the grace that is in Christ Jesus. The things which you have heard from me in the presence of many witnesses, entrust these to faithful men who will be able to teach others also."[18]

Another way we mentor by the design of the Holy Spirit is through celebrating baby dedication with parents. Paul recognized that he was not the first and only mentor in the life of Timothy. Writing to Timothy, Paul said:

> I thank God, whom I serve with a clear conscience the way my forefathers did, as I constantly remember you in my prayers night and day, longing to see you, even as I recall your tears, so that I may be filled with joy. For I am mindful of the sincere faith within you, which first dwelt in your grandmother Lois and your mother Eunice, and I am sure that it is in you as well.[19]

> You, however, continue in the things you have learned and become convinced of, knowing from whom you have learned them, and that from a childhood you have known the sacred writings which are able to give you the wisdom that leads to salvation through faith which is in Christ Jesus.[20]

Timothy's first mentors were his mother and grandmother. They led Timothy to know the Lord, love the Lord, and to love the Word of God. Paul built on the mentoring that Timothy has received at home. This is a powerful example of the role that we

18. 2 Timothy 2:1, 2.
19. 2 Timothy 1:3–5.
20. 2 Timothy 3:14, 15.

play as parents in raising our children. Proverbs 22:6 reminds us as parents to "train up a child in the way he should go, even when he is old he will not depart from it." Part of training our children is to mentor them in spiritual matters. We are to mentor our children to love the Lord, respect His Word, commune with God, walk according to the Spirit, and serve the Lord with their little hands and feet.

Mentoring begins at Home

When a baby is born, mother and father become the first spiritual mentors of their newborn baby. Yet when parents bring their child to church to be dedicated to God, the church also makes a commitment to become spiritual mentors for children and to foster an atmosphere of spiritual growth and discipleship. Therefore every baby dedication at church is an opportunity and privilege for the church to recommit themselves to the Lord as mentors.

Parents make the commitment to continue bringing their child to Jesus by praying daily for their child, by bringing the family together for morning and evening worship. Ellen White, the wife of James White, a great mentor of early Seventh-day Adventism said the following regarding Abraham and his role in leading and mentoring his family:

> Like the patriarchs of old, those who profess to love God should erect an altar to the Lord wherever they pitch their tent. If ever there was a time when every house should be a house of prayer, it is now. Father and mothers should often lift up their hearts to God in humble supplication for themselves and their children. Let the father, as priest of the household, lay upon the altar of God the morning and evening sacrifice, while the wife and children unite in prayer and praise. In such a household Jesus will love to tarry. From every Christian home a holy light should shine forth. Love should be revealed in action.[21]

21. White, *Prophets and Kings*, 144.

As parents, we pray daily, encourage, mentor our children and also make the commitment to bring them to church weekly, that the cradle roll teachers and primary teachers could also become mentors. We are to surround our children with positive, encouraging, Spirit-filled, prayer warriors, who will mentor our children to live for Christ. As parents, we also choose to become positive, encouraging, loving, Spirit-filled prayer warriors ourselves. We choose to become missional Christians, who live to be the hands and feet of Jesus and that we mentor our children to be missional Christians. Some ways we may include our children in missional living would be by feeding the hungry, singing to the elderly at nursing homes, making cards for the discouraged and sick, and a number of other ways that we could as families be the hands and feet of Jesus together.

I am thankful that my parents were the first mentors in my life and the lives of my brothers. Our parents were involved in church and in serving the Lord numerous ways. We traveled with our parents throughout different parts of Romania as they led out in sharing Christ through music. They instilled in us not only a love for music, but a love for God, for His Word, to serve, and praise the Lord.

Even though my father is asleep in Jesus awaiting the blessed hope of Christ's return, I will never forget the memory of how he would spend time with the Lord. My wife and I just began serving as a pastoral couple of a two church district in Cleveland, Ohio. Whenever we had vacation time, we would drive to visit our parents in Atlanta, Georgia. One Sunday evening we arrived in Atlanta and my father was getting ready to go to Alabama to do a job. I wanted to tag along and be with him in Alabama that week while Mariya stayed with her parents.

After working all day Monday, I was extremely tired and it did not take long to fall asleep that night. But early Tuesday morning, the lights came on in the room. My dad took out his Hungarian hymnal and sang a song, he studied his Sabbath School lesson, read his Bible, and then he knelt by his bed and prayed. The memory of him spending time with the Lord every morning that week left such a deep impression in my heart, that it changed the way I commune with God. He mentored me not only in living for God, but how to commune with the Lord also. As parents, let us take seriously the fact that we are to train and mentor our children to commune with Christ and to become missional Christians.

Chapter one began with all the mentors that God has placed in my life. We all could be thankful for the mentors that God has placed in all of our lives. I have shared with you some mentors that have been a Barnabas in my life. Just as Barnabas has mentored Paul, so God has placed individuals to be like Barnabas in our lives to mentor us. Who were the individuals that were like Barnabas in your life? Who were the great mentors that prayed for you and with you, who encouraged you, taught you to follow the Lord? What made them such great mentors?

Now, the Holy Spirit is inviting each one of us to be mentors in the life of others. For just as Barnabas mentored Paul, Paul went on to mentor Timothy. Who are the individuals that God has placed in your circle of influence that you are to mentor? Start by asking the Holy Spirit to impress upon you individuals to pray for. After much prayer, ask the Holy Spirit to lead you in mentoring someone through encouragement, support, and kindness. As parents, let us begin mentoring at home. As followers of Christ, let us mentor youth, young adults, and anyone the Holy Spirit places in our lives. And by the design of the Holy Spirit, and only by the design of the Holy Spirit, our mentoring will make a difference in the lives of others. And because effective mentoring is by the design of the Holy Spirit, the credit for effective mentoring does not belong to mentors. All praise, honor, and glory belong to God the Father, Jesus Christ, and the Holy Spirit.

Appendix A

Life Group Information Sheet and Leader Covenant

INFORMATION SHEET

What is the name of our group?

What is the Scripture of our group?

Who will be invited to be part of the group?

How many times we will meet in the next three months?

Group Leaders Name:

LEADER'S COVENANT

- I am in a covenant relationship with Mansfield Seventh-day Adventist Church and am currently a member or actively pursuing membership. I acknowledge the responsibilities of membership include regular worship attendance, involvement in a Life Group by leading or participating, tithing, taking advantage of educational opportunities for learning and discipleship as well as using my spiritual gifts to serve others.
- I promise to pray daily for the individuals in my group by name. (Matthew 7:7–8)
- I will live a lifestyle that is Christ honoring. (1 Thessalonians 5:22)
- I am committed to growing in my walk with God through daily devotion and listening to the guidance of the Holy Spirit in leading the Life Group.
- I will attend Life Group Training session for ongoing direction and support.
- I will do my best to identify and mentor a co-leader in my Life Group.
- I will contact the pastor when I am in need of prayer support or have a difficult situation in my Life Group for which I need guidance.

Printed Name____

Signature_____________________________Date ___________

Current Email Address ________________________________

Cell Phone ____

Home/Alternate Phone ________________________________

Appendix B

Sermon Series On Discipleship

First Sermon Series on discipleship was based on Glenn McDonald's book, The Disciple Making Church:[1]

1. January 11, 2014 "Who is your Lord?"
2. January 18, 2014 "Who am I?"
3. February 8, 2014 "Barnabas and Timothy"
4. February 15, 2014 "Where is your Antioch?"
5. February 22, 2014 "Where is your Macedonia?
6. March 1, 2014 "Cost of Discipleship"

Second sermon series was on the life's of the disciples of Jesus:

1. March 8, 2014 "Peter"
2. March 22, 2014 "Andrew"
3. April 5, 2014 "James, the brother of John"
4. April, 12, 2014 "John"
5. April 19, 2014 "Thomas"
6. April 26, 2014 "James, the Son of Alpheus"
7. May 17, 2014 "Simon the Zealot"
8. May 24, 2014 "Philip"
9. June 21, 2014 "Nathanael (also known as Bartholomew)"
10. June 28, 2014 "Matthew"
11. August 2, 2014 "Judas (also known as Thaddeus, Labbaeus) "
12. August 9, 2014 "Judas Iscariot"
13. August 16, 2014 "Mary and Martha"

1. Glenn McDonald, *The Disciple Making Church* (Grand Haven, MI: FaithWalk Publishing, 2007).

Next sermon series was on discipleship through missional small groups based on the book *Missional Small Groups* by M. Scott Boren:[2]

1. September 6, 2014 "Why Missional Small Groups?"
2. September 13, 2014 "Characteristics of Missional Small Groups"
3. September 20, 2014 "Loving God through Missional Small Groups"
4. September 27, 2014 "Loving one another through Missional Small Groups"
5. October 4, 2014 "Loving the community through Missional Small Groups"

Last sermon series on discipleship was on the thought of almost disciples and faithful discipleship based on the parable of the sower and seed (Matthew 13:1–9, 18–23):

1. November 1, 2014 "Seed by the wayside"
2. November 8, 2014 "Seed by stony places"
3. November 15, 2014 "Seed by thorns"
4. December 6, 2014 "Seed on good ground"

2. M. Scott Boren, *Missional Small Groups* (Grand Rapids, MI: BakerBooks, 2010).

Bibliography

Amit, Yairah. "A Prophet Tested: Elisha, the Great Woman of Shunem, and the Story's Double Message." Biblical Interpretation 11, (2003) 279–94.

Andrews, Alan, ed. *The Kingdom Life*. Colorado Springs, CO: NavPress, 2010.

Arnold, Clinton E., ed. *John, Acts*. Zondervan Illustrated Bible Backgrounds Commentary, vol. 2. Grand Rapids: Zondervan, 2002.

Attridge, Harold W., ed. *Harper Collins Study Bible*. New York: HarperOne, 2006.

Baliles, Mark E. *Acts of the Apostles*. Brethren New Testament Commentary. Ephrata, PA: Brethren Revival Fellowship, 2010.

Barclay, William. *The Master's Men*. New York: Abingdon, 1959.

Boren, M Scott. *Missional Small Groups*. Grand Rapids: Baker Books, 2010.

Brueggemann, Walter. *1 & 2 Kings*. Smyth & Helwys Bible Commentary. Macon, GA: Smyth & Helwys, 2000.

Bruinsma, Reinder. *The Body of Christ*. Hagerstown, MD: Review and Herald, 2009.

Chance, J. Bradley. *Acts*. Smyth & Helwys Bible Commentary. Macon, GA: Smyth & Helwys, 2007.

Clayburn, P., et al. "Promoting Social Support: Peer Mentoring in a Baccalaureate Nursing Program." Paper presented at the University of New Mexico Mentoring Institute, October 31, 2013, Albuquergue, NM.

Cogan, Mordechai, and Hayim Tadmor. *II Kings*. The Anchor Yale Bible. New Haven: Yale University Press, 1988.

Cohn, Robert L. *2 Kings*. Berit Olam. Collegeville, MN: The Liturgical, 2000.

Cole, Neil. *Organic Leadership*. Grand Rapids: Baker Books, 2009.

Coleman, Robert E. *The Master Plan of Evangelism*, 30th Anniversary ed. Grand Rapids: Fleming H. Revell, 1972.

Coogan, Michael D., ed. *The New Oxford Annotated Bible*, 3rd ed. New York: Oxford University Press, 2007.

Cordle, Steve. *The Church in Many Houses*. Nashville, TN: Abingdon, 2005.

Cranton, Patricia. *Professional Development as Transformative Learning*. San Francisco, CA: Jossey-Bass, 1996.

Creach, Jerome F. D. *Violence in Scripture*. Interpretation. Louisville, KY: Westminster John Knox, 2013.

Crow, D. Michael. "Multiplying Jesus Mentors: Designing a Reproducible Mentoring System: A Case Study." *Missiology* 36, no. 1 (January 1, 2008) 87–109.

Dennison, Susan. "Peer Mentoring: Untapped Potential." *Journal of Nursing Education* Vol. 49, no. 6 (2010) 340–342.

Dybdahl, Jon L., ed. *Andrews Study Bible*. Berrien Springs, MI: Andrews University Press, 2010.

Fischer, Roland E. "Mentoring Interns and Young Pastors." *Ministry*, September, 2014.

Foster, Frances. "Andrews & His Family." *Lest We Forget*, Second Quarter, vol. 6, no. 2 (1996) 6–7.

Fritz, Volkmar. *1 & 2 Kings*. A Continental Commentary. Translated by Anselm Hagedorn. Minneapolis: Fortress, 2003.

Froom, LeRoy E. *The Coming of the Comforter*, rev. ed. Washington DC: Review and Herald, 1956.

Frost, Michael. *Exiles*. Peabody, MA: Hendrickson, 2006.

———. *The Road to Missional*. Grand Rapids: BakerBooks, 2011.

Garrett, Duane A., ed., *Archaeological Study Bible*. Grand Rapids: Zondervan, 2010.

Gaventa, Beverly Roberts. *Acts*. Abingdon New Testament Commentaries. Nashville: Abingdon, 2003.

George, Timothy, ed. *Acts*. Reformation Commentary on Scripture. Downers Grove, IL: IVP Academic, 2014.

Gilmour, Jean A., Anna Kopeikin, and Jeanie Douche. "Student Nurses as Peer-mentors: Collegiality in Practice." *Nurse Education in Practice* 7 (2007) 36–43.

Green, Joel B. *The Gospel of Luke*. The New International Commentary on the New Testament. Grand Rapids: Eerdmans, 1997.

Grenz, Stanley J. *Theology for the Community of God*. Grand Rapids: Eerdmans, 2000.

Hall, Ralph, and Zarni Jaugietis. "Developing Peer Mentoring through Evaluation." 3 August 2010. http://link.springer.com/article/10.1007/s10755-010-9156-6

Hardinge, Leslie. *Ambassadors*, 2nd ed. Harrisburg, PA: American Cassette Ministries, Book Division, 2004.

Hens-Piazza, Gina. 1–2 *Kings*. Abingdon Old Testament Commentaries. Nashville: Abingdon, 2006.

Hirsch, Alan. *The Forgotten Ways*. Grand Rapids: BrazosPress, 2006.

Hunter, James Davison. *To Change the World*. New York, NY: Oxford University Press, 2010.

Hull, Bill. *The Complete Book of Discipleship*. Colorado Springs, CO: NavPress, 2006.

Inbody, Tyron. *The Faith of the Christian Church.* Grand Rapids: Eerdmans, 2005.

Johnson, W. Brad, and Charles R. Ridley. *The Elements of Mentoring.* New York, NY: Palgrace Macmillan, 2004.

Keller, Timothy. *Center Church.* Grand Rapids: Zondervan, 2012.

Kidder, S. Joseph. *The Big Four.* Hagerstown, MD: Review and Herald, 2011.

Kinnaman, David. *You Lost Me.* Grand Rapids: Baker, 2011.

Knight, George. *Ellen White's World.* Hagerstown, MD: Review and Herald, 1998.

———. *Joseph Bates.* Hagerstown, MD: Review and Herald, 2004.

———. *Lest We Forget.* Hagerstown, MD: Review and Herald, 2008.

———. *Meeting Ellen White.* Hagerstown, MD: Review and Herald, 1996.

———. *Walking With Ellen White.* Hagerstown, MD: Review and Herald, 1999.

Konkel, August H. *1 & 2 Kings.* The NIV Application Commentary. Grand Rapids: Zondervan, 2006.

LaHaye, Beveryly. "How Christians Make an Impact on Their Government." In *Citizen Christians: The Rights and Responsibilities of Dual Citizenship,* edited by Richard D. Land and Louis A. Moore, ch. 10. Nashville, TN: Broadman and Holman, 1994.

LaSor, William Sanford, David Allan Hubbard, Frederic Wm. Bush. *Old Testament Survey,* 2nd ed. Grand Rapids: Eerdmans, 1996.

Leithart, Peter J. *1 & 2 Kings.* Brazos Theological Commentary on the Bible. Grand Rapids: Brazos, 2006.

Leonard, Harry, ed. *J. N. Andrews: The Man and the Mission.* Berrien Springs, MI: Andrews University Press, 1985.

Levine, Nachman. "Twice as Much of Your Spirit: Pattern, Parallel and Paronomasia in the Miracles of Elijah and Elisha." *Journal For The Study Of The Old Testament* 85 (1999) 25–46.

Li, H-C., L. S. Wang, Y-H. Lin, I. Lee. "The effect of a peer-mentoring strategy on student nurse sress reduction in clinical practice." *International Nursing Review* (2010) 203–10.

Ludemann, Gerd. *The Acts of the Apostles.* Amherst, NY: Prometheus, 2005.

MacArthur, John. *Twelve Ordinary Men.* Nashville, TN: Thomas Nelson, 2002.

Macchia, Frank D. *Baptized in the Spirit.* Grand Rapids: Zondervan, 2006.

Malina, Bruce J., and John J. Pilch. *Social-Science Commentary on the Book of Acts.* Minneapolis: Fortress, 2008.

Martynov, Vitaliy. "The Elements of Mentoring." *Christian Education Journal* 3, no. 2 (September 1, 2006) 429–33.

Maxwell, C Mervyn. *Tell it to the World.* Nampa, ID: Pacific Press, 1976.

McDonald, Glenn. *The Disciple Making Church.* Grand Haven, MI: FaithWalk, 2007.

Ministerial Association General Council, *Seventh-day Adventists Believe,* 2nd ed. Boise, ID: Pacific Press, 2005.

Moltmann, Jürgen. *The Source of Life.* Minneapolis, MN: Fortress, 1997.

Nichol, Francis D. ed,. "Joshua to 2 Kings." *Seventh-day Adventist Bible Commentary*, 7 vols. Washington DC: Review and Herald, 1954.

———. "Acts to Ephesians." *Seventh-day Adventist Bible Commentary*, 7 vols. Washington DC: Review and Herald, 1957.

Ogden, Greg. *Discipleship Essentials*. Downers Grove, IL: InterVarsity, 1998.

Parsons, Mikeal C. *Acts*. Paideia Commentaries on the New Testament. Grand Rapids: Baker Academic, 2008.

Paulsen, Jan. "The Holy Spirit—So What?" *Ministry (*April, 2012) 8.

Pelikan, Jaroslav. *Acts*. Brazos Theological Commentary on the Bible. Grand Rapids: Brazos, 2005.

Pervo, Richard I. *Acts*. Hermeneia. Minneapolis: Fortress, 2009.

Peterson, David G. *The Acts of the Apostles*. The Pillar New Testament Commentary. Grand Rapids: Eerdmans, 2009.

"The Priorities, Challenges, and Trends in Youth Ministry." Barna Group, 2016. https://www.barna.org/research/leaders-pastors/research-release/the-priorities-challenges-and-trends-in-youth-ministry#.V2sPPJMrKb9.

Provan, Iain. *1 & 2 Kings, 1 & 2 Chronicles, Ezra, Nehemiah, Esther*. 5 vols. Zondervan Illustrated Bible Backgrounds Commentary: Old Testament Set, edited by John H. Walton. Grand Rapids: Zondervan, 2009.

Rice, Richard. *The Reign of God*. Berrien Springs, MI: Andrews University Press, 1997.

Rius-Camps, Josep, and Jenny Read-Heimerdinger. *The Message of Acts in Codex Bezae*. vol. 2. *Acts 6.1–12.25: From Judaea and Samaria to the Church in Antioch*. New York: T & T Clark, 2006.

Robinson, Erin, and Louise Niemer. "A Peer Mentor Tutor Program for Academic Success in Nursing." *Nursing Education Perspectives* vol. 31, no. 5 (2010) 286–89.

Robinson, Virgil. *James White*. Hagerstown, MD: Review and Herald, 1976.

———. *John Nevins Andrews: Flame for the Lord*. Washington DC: Review and Herald, 1975.

Roxburgh, Alan J. *Missional: Joining God in the Neighborhood*. Grand Rapids: BakerBooks, 2011.

Scott, Elaine S. "Peer-to-Peer Mentoring: Teaching Collegiality." *Nurse Educator*, vol. 30, no. 2 (2005) 52–56.

Scott, Steven K. *The Greatest Words Ever Spoken*. Colorado Springs, CO: WaterBrook, 2008

Seitzer, Christopher R., ed. *Nicene Christianity: The Future for a New Ecumenism*. Grand Rapids: Brazos, 2001.

Shields, Mary E. "Subverting a Man of God, Elevating a Woman: Role and Power Reversals in 2 Kings 4." *Journal For The Study Of The Old Testament* 58 (1993) 59–69.

Slaughter, Mike. *Change the World*. Nashville, TN: Abingdon, 2010.

———. *Dare to Dream*. Nashville, TN: Abingdon, 2013.

———. *Momentum for Life*. Revised ed. Nashville, TN: Abingdon, 2008.

———. *Spiritual Entrepreneurs*. Nashville, TN: Abingdon, 1994.

Smoot, J. G. "The Churchman: Andrews' Relationship With Church Leaders." In Harry Leondard, ed. *J. N. Andrews: The Man and the Mission*, 42–74. Berrien Springs, MI: Andrews University Press, 1985.

Solis, Dan. *Discipleship*. Nampa, ID: Pacific Press, 2014.

Steinweg, Marlene. "J. N. Andrews: In Defense of the Truth." *Adventist Pioneer Library: Lest We Forget,* 2nd Quarter (1996) 1, 4, 5.

Steveny, Georges. "Andrews' Peronal Library." In Harry Leondard, ed. *J. N. Andrews: The Man and the Mission*, 148–49. Berrien Springs, MI: Andrews University Press, 1985.

Stott, John. *Baptism and Fullness*, 3rd ed. Downers Grove, IL: IVP, 2006.

———. *Life in Christ*. Grand Rapids: Baker, 2003.

Tannehill, R. C. "'Cornelius' and 'Tabitha' Encounter Luke's Jesus." *Interpretation* 48, no. 4 (1994): 347–56.

Thompson, Christopher C. *360° Christian*. Lincoln, NE: AdventSource, 2012.

Vickers, Jason E. *Minding the Good Ground*. Waco, TX: Baylor University Press, 2011.

Wheeler, Gerald. *James White*. Hagerstown, MD: Review and Herald, 2003.

White, Arthur L. *Ellen G. White: The Early Years*, 6 vols. Hagerstown, MD: Review and Herald, 1985.

———. *Ellen G. White: The Progressive Years*, 6 vols. Hagerstown, MD: Review and Herald, 1985.

———. *Ellen G. White: The Lonely Years*, 6 vols. Hagerstown, MD: Review and Herald, 1985.

White, Ellen G. *Acts of the Apostles*. Boise, ID: Pacific Press, 1911.

———. *Patriarchs and Prophets*. Boise, ID: Pacific Press, 1890.

———. *Prophets and Kings*. Boise, ID: Pacific Press, 1917.

Willimon, William H. *Acts*. Interpretation. Louisville, KY: John Knox, 1988.

Zuck, Roy B. *Spirit-Filled Teaching*. Nashville, TN: Word, 1998.

Zucker, David J. "Elijah and Elisha. Part 2, Similarities and Differences." *Jewish Bible Quarterly* 41, no. 1 (January 1, 2013) 19–23.

www.ingramcontent.com/pod-product-compliance
Lightning Source LLC
LaVergne TN
LVHW010932100826
845153LV00001B/8

* 9 7 8 1 4 9 8 2 9 4 2 9 4 *